The

Australian
Cattle Dog

An Owner's Guide To

A HAPPY HEALTHY PET

Howell Book House

Howell Book House
A Simon & Schuster Macmillan Company
1633 Broadway
New York, NY 10019

Macmillan Publishing books may be purchased for business or sales promotional use.
For information please write: Special Markets Department, Macmillan Publishing
USA, 1633 Broadway, New York, NY 10019.

MACMILLAN is a registered trademark of Macmillan, Inc.

Library of Congress Cataloging-in-Publication Data
Buetow, Katherine.
The Australian cattle dog: an owner's guide to a happy, healthy pet / Katherine Buetow.
p. cm.
ISBN **978-1-63056-052-1**
Library of congress cataloging-in-publication data available upon request.
Manufactured in the United States of America
10 9 8 7 6 5 4 3 2 1

Series Director: Amanda Pisani
Series Assistant Director: Jennifer Liberts
Book Design by Michele Laseau
Cover Design by Iris Jeromnimon
Illustration by Marvin Van Tiem and Jeff Yesh
Photography:
 Front cover by Charles Mercer and back cover by Katherine Buetow
 Paulette Braun (Pets by Paulette): 5, 11, 50, 62, 64, 65
 Katherine Buetow: 2–3, 8, 17, 29, 32, 34, 40, 43, 55, 61, 71, 79, 92
 M. Kathleen Buetow: 72
 Deb Casey: i
 Lori Herbel: 30
 Louis Hizer: 23
 Lena Holm: 25
 Melissa Hotter: 73
 Gary Loescher: 41, 57, 68, 69
 Marilyn Painter: 10
 Judith E. Strom: 13, 15, 18, 42, 52
 John Thomas: 33
 Faith Uridel: 9, 20, 27
 Jean Wentworth: 46
 Lori Whitman: 38–39
Production Team: Stephanie Hammett, Natalie Hollifield, Clint Lahnen,
Stephanie Mohler, Dennis Sheehan, Terri Sheehan

Contents

Welcome to the World

of the

Australian
Cattle Dog

External Features of the Australian Cattle Dog

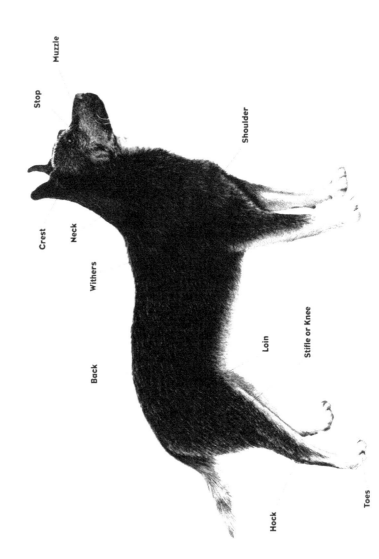

Stop

Muzzle

Crest

Neck

Shoulder

Withers

Back

Loin

Stifle or Knee

Hock

Toes

chapter 1

What Is an Australian Cattle Dog?

Welcome to the wonderful world of the Australian Cattle Dog. Whether you already share your life with one or are just beginning to investigate these dogs, you are sure to find the breed to be one of the most unique and intelligent members of the canine family. The Australian Cattle Dog is both physically and mentally energetic, fiercely loyal, comically entertaining and above all an incredible companion.

The History of the Breed

The breed is often referred to as the Queensland Heeler, or the Blue or Red Heeler. Both names summarize its heritage and function.

5

The breed was developed near Queensland, Australia in the mid- to late 1800s as a driving dog that nipped at the heels of livestock to keep them moving (hence the term "heeler"). The final combination of dogs used in the development of the breed gave us the two colors of Australian Cattle Dog, red and blue (see chapter 2).

The Breed Standard

One good way to learn about this breed, and why it was bred to look and act as it does, is to review the American Kennel Club (AKC) Breed Standard. Think of the standard as a recipe for the ideal Australian Cattle Dog. Much of the breed standard refers to pure working traits. However, though the breed was developed for herding, most of these traits are also desirable for other reasons. What follow are excerpts from the Australian Cattle Dog standard. Since breed standards can be somewhat confusing at times, in each section I have included a commentary to clarify meaning.

YOU'VE GOT THE LOOK!

General Appearance *The general appearance is that of a sturdy, compact, symmetrically-built working dog. With the ability and willingness to carry out any task, however arduous, its combination of substance, power, balance, and hard, muscular condition to be such that must convey the impression of great agility, strength, and endurance. Any tendency to grossness or weediness is a serious fault.*

Above all, the Australian Cattle Dog is a working dog that must be physically capable of doing the work of many men. Balance is the key in looking at an Australian Cattle Dog—both grossness (bulkiness) and weediness (lightness of bone or legginess) detract from an overall symmetrically built dog and will lead to a lack of stamina.

Head *The head, in balance with other proportions of the dog, and in keeping with its general conformation, is broad of skull and only slightly curved between the ears, flattening to a slight but definite stop. The cheeks are muscular, but not coarse nor prominent, the underjaw is strong, deep and* *well-developed. The foreface is broad and well filled in under the eye, tapering gradually to a medium length, deep and powerful muzzle. The lips are tight and clean. The nose is black irrespective of the color of the dog.*

The Australian Cattle Dog grips low on the heels of stock to get them moving, a tactic that is often followed by a swift backward kick from the livestock. While a good working Australian Cattle Dog should be quick and sensible enough to get out of harm's way in an instant, the head of an Australian Cattle Dog at work often takes a few blows. When an Australian Cattle Dog uses the proper techniques, his head is directly in the line of fire, so it must be a head that is strong, sturdy and powerful enough to take a kick when necessary.

Teeth *The teeth should be sound, strong, and regularly spaced, gripping with a scissors-like action, the lower incisors close behind and just touching the upper. Not to be undershot nor overshot.*

The jaw, like the head, must be able to take the shock of a hoof. An improperly aligned bite, lack of underjaw or missing teeth will weaken the jaw and increase the chance of serious injury to the dog while he is working.

Eyes *The eyes should be oval shaped of medium size, neither prominent nor sunken, and must express alertness and intelligence. A warning or suspicious glint is characteristic. Eye color is dark brown.*

The Australian Cattle Dog's eyes are vitally important to his function. The vision of an independent working dog must be acute and unhindered. Prominent eyes will tend to be injured by a flying hoof or by underbrush. Eyes that are sunken have potential for gathering dust and dirt while working.

Ears *The ears should be of moderate size, preferably small rather than large, broad at the base, muscular, pricked, and moderately pointed (not spoon nor bat eared). Set wide apart on the skull, inclined outwards, sensitive in their use, and firmly erect when alert. The inside of the ear should be well furnished with hair.*

*A strong neck
is essential to
a properly con-
formed Austra-
lian Cattle Dog.*

The size of the Australian Cattle Dog's ears should be in proportion to his head and body. His ears should be sensitive and inclined outwards to aid him in hearing a handler's command from a distance. The hair on the inside of his ears will protect them from gathering debris that could lead to discomfort or infection.

Neck *The neck is of exceptional strength, muscular, and of medium length, broadening to blend into the body and free from throatiness.*

The Australian Cattle Dog's neck carries the head of the dog as he nips at and avoids livestock. A neck that is too short will lack range of motion and a neck that is too long will delay reaction time and possibly put the dog in the path of a kick.

Forequarters *The shoulders are broad of blade, sloping, muscular, and well angulated to the upper arm, and at the point of the withers should not be too closely set. The forelegs have strong round bone, extending to the feet without weakness at the pasterns. The forelegs should be perfectly straight viewed from the front, but the pasterns should show a slight angle with the forearm when regarded from the side.*

The Australian Cattle Dog is required to cover great distances with minimal effort. There are ideal angles and proportions in the assembly of the body and limbs that provide the Australian Cattle Dog with the physical *well-developed. The foreface is broad and well filled in under the eye, tapering gradually to a medium length, deep and powerful muzzle. The lips are tight and clean. The nose is black irrespective of the color of the dog.*

The Australian Cattle Dog grips low on the heels of stock to get them moving, a tactic that is often followed by a swift backward kick from the livestock. While a good working Australian Cattle Dog should be quick and sensible enough to get out of harm's way in an instant, the head of an Australian Cattle Dog at work often takes a few blows. When an Australian Cattle Dog uses the proper techniques, his head is directly in the line of fire, so it must be a head that is strong, sturdy and powerful enough to take a kick when necessary.

Teeth   *The teeth should be sound, strong, and regularly spaced, gripping with a scissors-like action, the lower incisors close behind and just touching the upper. Not to be undershot nor overshot.*

The jaw, like the head, must be able to take the shock of a hoof. An improperly aligned bite, lack of underjaw or missing teeth will weaken the jaw and increase the chance of serious injury to the dog while he is working.

Eyes   *The eyes should be oval shaped of medium size, neither prominent nor sunken, and must express alertness and intelligence. A warning or suspicious glint is characteristic. Eye color is dark brown.*

The Australian Cattle Dog's eyes are vitally important to his function. The vision of an independent working dog must be acute and unhindered. Prominent eyes will tend to be injured by a flying hoof or by underbrush. Eyes that are sunken have potential for gathering dust and dirt while working.

Ears   *The ears should be of moderate size, preferably small rather than large, broad at the base, muscular, pricked, and moderately pointed (not spoon nor bat eared). Set wide apart on the skull, inclined outwards, sensitive in their use, and firmly erect when alert. The inside of the ear should be well furnished with hair.*

The size of the Australian Cattle Dog's ears should be in proportion to his head and body. His ears should be sensitive and inclined outwards to aid him in hearing a handler's command from a distance. The hair on the inside of his ears will protect them from gathering debris that could lead to discomfort or infection.

A strong neck is essential to a properly conformed Australian Cattle Dog.

Neck *The neck is of exceptional strength, muscular, and of medium length, broadening to blend into the body and free from throatiness.*

The Australian Cattle Dog's neck carries the head of the dog as he nips at and avoids livestock. A neck that is too short will lack range of motion and a neck that is too long will delay reaction time and possibly put the dog in the path of a kick.

Forequarters *The shoulders are broad of blade, sloping, muscular, and well angulated to the upper arm, and at the point of the withers should not be too closely set. The forelegs have strong round bone, extending to the feet without weakness at the pasterns. The forelegs should be perfectly straight viewed from the front, but the pasterns should show a slight angle with the forearm when regarded from the side.*

The Australian Cattle Dog is required to cover great distances with minimal effort. There are ideal angles and proportions in the assembly of the body and limbs that provide the Australian Cattle Dog with the physical advantage to work for many hours without tiring. For best advantage, the upper arm should join the shoulder at a 90° angle. The slight angle of the pasterns is necessary to absorb the shock of running and jumping. Too much angulation in the pastern will cause weakness in the dog's legs. Too little will lead to the entire front end of the dog being jarred, and thus strained with repetitive movement.

Hindquarters *The hindquarters are broad, sloping and muscular. The rump is rather long and sloping, thighs long, broad and well developed, with moderate turn to stifle. The hocks are strong and well let down. When viewed from behind, the hind legs, from the hocks to the feet, are straight and placed neither close nor too wide apart.*

The rear legs provide the driving force of the Australian Cattle Dog's movement. A long, sloping croup coupled with a moderate turn to stifle provides room for the proper angulation of the hip and knee. The rear pasterns (the hocks) are to be short and should be perpendicular to the ground when at rest.

As a working dog, the Australian Cattle Dog must have strong forequarters and hindquarters.

Feet *The feet should be round and the toes short, strong, well-arched and held together. The pads hard and deep, and the nails must be short and strong.*

The Australian Cattle Dog relies on a functional foot to carry him through his work. Splayed or otherwise weak feet will allow pebbles or burrs to lodge between the pads. Hard, deep pads are required for travel over rough terrain.

Body *The length of the body from the point of the breast bone, in a straight line to the buttocks, is greater than the height at the withers, as 10 is to 9. The topline is level, back strong, with ribs well sprung and ribbed back. (Not barrel ribbed.) The chest is deep and muscular, and moderately* *broad, loins are broad, deep and muscular with deep flanks strongly coupled between the fore and hindquarters.*

The proportion of ten to nine is the ideal length to height ratio that makes movement the most energy efficient. This proportion also allows for the quick movement of the Australian Cattle Dog toward stock or away from danger. The rib cage needs to provide ample room for the heart, and room for the lungs to expand to their full capacity during work.

The tail is an important part of a Cattle Dog's body and is necessary for safe herding.

Tail   *The set of the tail is low, following the contours of the sloping rump, and at rest should hang in a slight curve of a length to reach approximately to the hock. During movement and/or excitement it may be raised, but under no circumstances should any part of the tail be carried past a vertical line drawn through the root.*

The tail of the Australian Cattle Dog acts as a rudder, providing balance for the dog while he's moving. A heeling dog needs to be able to literally turn on a dime as he nips and ducks flying hooves. The tail is a vital part of the Australian Cattle Dog's movement and should never be docked.

Coat   *The weather resisting outer coat is moderately short, straight and of medium texture, with short dense undercoat. Behind the quarters the coat is longer, forming a mild breeching. The tail is furnished sufficiently to form a good brush.*

The head, forelegs, hind legs from hock to ground, are coated with short hair.

The Australian Cattle Dog is asked to work in all weather conditions—rain or shine, hot or cold. The coat of the Australian Cattle Dog provides protection from all of the elements, is resistant to many burrs and does not allow branches or scrub to penetrate and scratch the skin.

Color (Blue) *The color should be blue or blue-mottled with or without other markings. The permissible markings are black, blue or tan markings on the head, evenly distributed for preference. The forelegs tan midway up the legs and extending up the front to the breast and throat, with tan on jaws; the hindquarters tan on inside of hind legs, and inside of thighs, showing down the front of the stifles and broadening out to the outside of the hind legs from hock to toes. Tan under coat is permissible on the body provided it does not show through the blue outer coat. Black markings on the body are not desirable.*

A red speckle Cattle Dog with a blue puppy.

Color (Red Speckle) *The color should be a good even red speckle all over including the undercoat (not white or cream) with or without darker red markings on the head. Even head markings are desirable. Red markings on the body are permissible but not desirable.*

The colors of the Australian Cattle Dog come from the red of the Dingo and the blue merle of the Highland Collie (See chapter 2). The variation in both the red

11

and the blue coloring is often extreme. The blue Australian Cattle Dogs range from a silvery color to almost completely black. The red Australian Cattle Dogs are somewhere between light orange and a deep rust color. While body spots are discouraged in the breed standard, a spot at the root of the tail is viewed historically as a "utility mark," which has been traced back to some of the early, great dogs in the breed. In the past, Australian Cattle Dogs that bore this spot were highly prized and said to have the best herding ability. However, primary focus should be on the way an animal is built and not on his color or extraneous markings. Of historical significance, but not mentioned in the standard, is the white blaze that most Australian Cattle Dogs carry on their foreheads. This is known as a "Bentley mark" in honor of the Australian settler Thomas Bentley, whose widely used stud dog is reported to have passed along this trait.

Size *The desirable height at the withers to be within the following dimensions: Dogs 18 to 20 inches. Bitches 17 to 19 inches. Dogs or bitches over or under these specified sizes are undesirable.*

The standard lays out the ideal height for the breed as ranging from 17 to 20 inches. The Australian Cattle Dog should be a moderate breed in all respects—height included. A dog who is too small will require more effort to cover the same distance than his larger counterpart. A dog who is too large will also require more effort for movement and will have a more difficult time avoiding the kicks of irate livestock.

All the Right Moves

Movement *Soundness is of paramount importance. The action is true, free, supple and tireless, the movement of the shoulders and forelegs with the powerful thrust of the hindquarters, in unison. Capability of quick and sudden movement is essential. Stillness, loaded or slack shoulders, straight shoulder placement, weakness at elbows, pasterns or feet, straight stifles, cow or bow hocks, must be regarded as serious faults.*

Whether slightly high on the leg, a little straight in the stifle or just outside of the height standards, the correct Australian Cattle Dog is one that can carry himself through a day of arduous work without tiring. Balance and moderation are the key words in describing type in the Australian Cattle Dog. While description of the "work" of the Australian Cattle Dog often revolves around herding cattle or sheep, remember that the same stamina and capability of sudden movement are necessary for playing Frisbee or chasing a tennis ball—two activities in which this breed excels.

THE DOG'S PERSONALITY

Characteristics *The utility purpose is assistance in the control of cattle, in both wide open and confined areas. Ever alert, extremely intelligent, watchful, courageous, and trustworthy, with an implicit devotion to duty, making it an ideal dog. Its loyalty and protective instincts make a self-appointed guardian to the stockman, his herd, and his property. Whilst suspicious of strangers, must be amenable to handling in the show ring.*

Even a friendly Australian Cattle Dog will get rough-and-tough when it comes to protecting his owner.

The preceding paragraph well describes the personality of a typical Australian Cattle Dog. Though many Australian Cattle Dogs will seem like the friendliest of companions, they are extremely sensitive to the emotions of their owners, and so will defend their person and their property if they feel it necessary. The Australian Cattle Dog is extremely intelligent, often making it a less than ideal choice for a first-time dog owner. Their cunning minds are easily bored with ordinary routines and their brains need to be constantly challenged to keep them happy.

13

Unfortunately, Australian Cattle Dogs that are raised outside a home environment or poorly socialized as puppies sometimes show aggressive tendencies. The Australian Cattle Dog temperament should be reserved towards strangers and suspicious of those who are possibly threatening to their owners or their property, but should never be overtly aggressive.

Nobody's Perfect

Keep in mind that there is no such thing as the "perfect" Australian Cattle Dog. The standard describes the ideal build and makeup for the breed. As I always say, the perfect Australian Cattle Dog is the one that is curled up at my feet right now! That is how everyone should feel about his or her Australian Cattle Dog.

chapter 2

The **Australian Cattle Dog's Ancestry**

The Australian Cattle Dog is a relatively new breed and because of this, numerous records have been kept on its development. The writings of Mr. Robert Kaleski, who fell in love with the breed at the age of sixteen, and who spent his entire life breeding and studying the Australian

Cattle Dog, are invaluable for researching the development of the breed in its native Australia.

Where Did the Australian Cattle Dog Come From?

Despite the availability of documents like Kaleski's, there is a continuing controversy over which breeds were actually used in the Australian Cattle Dog's development. One of the difficulties in researching the history of the breed is that a lot of experimentation went on in trying to find the perfect combination of dogs to make up the ultimate heeler who could live and work in the Australian outback. While it is said that certain breeds were tried as a cross and subsequently found unsuitable (the Bull Terrier being the most notable), it does not appear that all progeny of that experiment were truly taken out of all the breeding programs. Another problem lies in the meaning of the names used for breeds in the past versus the names that we use today. For example, a "Collie" in the mid-1800s was not the "Lassie-dog" that we think of today when we hear the word "Collie." This factor has led to a lot of confusion in the translation of early writings.

The Need for Stamina

The early settlers in Australia brought with them both livestock and the dogs that they used in work. These Sheepdog-type canines were wonderful herders in the British Isles, but they were not built to withstand the rigors of the rugged Australian outback. These dogs were known as "Smithfields," a name taken from the central Smithfield meat markets of London. Smithfields were generally described as heavy, black, flop-eared, bobtailed dogs with white around the neck and sometimes on the tip of the tail or on the feet. These dogs were decent herders, but their heavy coats and bulk resulted in a lack of stamina when the colonizers moved inland, toward the harsher climates of the outback. Ranchers complained that the Smithfield's bite was too severe and rustlers complained that they were too noisy when working.

The first attempt at breeding a Cattle Dog suitable for the conditions in Australia came from a man by the name of Timmins, who decided to cross the Smithfield with the native Australian Dingo. A man known to occasionally "borrow his neighbors' cattle," Timmins was eager to breed a silent working dog. The resulting dogs were a red bobtailed breed that became known as "Timmins Biters," and they were indeed silent workers.

Unfortunately, the name was fitting, and it was quickly discovered that these dogs were severe biters who could very well kill calves when out of their owner's sight.

The next breed that the ranchers tried crossing with the Dingo was the purebred rough Collie. It was found that these dogs had a tendency to bark at the head of cattle and work them into a frenzy. This became a particular concern when the feeder cattle started coming to market several pounds lighter than they should have been because of all the extra exercise.

The Australian Cattle Dog was bred to be a heeling dog.

HALL'S HEELERS

In 1840, Mr. Thomas Hall of Muswelbrook, New South Wales imported a couple of Blue Smooth Highland Collies. These dogs were not the rough or smooth Collies we think of today. They have been described as blue merle dogs, similar to either the modern Border or Bearded Collies. These Blue Smooth Highland Collies were a bit better than the previous herding dogs that had been tried, but they still had the tendency to go for the cattle's heads. Mr. Hall took the progeny of these two Collies and crossed them with the Dingo. The resulting dogs were either blue or red speckled pups that became known as "Hall's Heelers." These dogs, described as blue or red thickset Dingoes, crept up on livestock silently, nipped and then would immediately "clap," or flatten to the ground, to avoid the backlashing kick of an angry bovine. Mr. Hall continued his experimental Highland Collie–Dingo breedings until his death in 1870.

THOMAS BENTLEY'S DOG

Mr. Tom Bentley's dog was said to have been of the pure Hall strain and was both beautifully built and an incredible worker. Bentley's Dog (known by only that name) was reportedly widely used at stud (meaning, he

was used in breeding) to retain these outstanding characteristics. It is said that the white blaze seen on the forehead of all Australian Cattle Dogs today and the black tail-root spot seen occasionally in blue dogs can be directly attributed to Tom Bentley's Dog.

MORE NEW BLOOD

Word spread of these Hall's Heelers, now also referred to as "Blue Heelers" or "Queensland Heelers," and in the early 1870s a butcher named Fred Davis brought a pair of

It is believed that the white forehead blaze that appears in the breed comes from a common ancestor called Tom Bentley's Dog.

Hall's dogs to work in the stockyards of Sydney. It was there that Mr. Davis and his colleagues infused a bit of Bull Terrier's blood into the dogs for added tenacity. These dogs were gradually phased out of the breeding programs because they were said to grip the cattle and not let go, and because they had limited mobility due to their stocky build. The Bull Terrier's influence is occasionally evident even in today's Australian Cattle Dogs.

THE BROTHERS BAGUST

Two brothers, Jack and Harry Bagust, took the Hall's Heelers in another direction. They bred a Hall's Heeler bitch to an imported Dalmatian, with the intent of instilling the love for horses and faithfulness to their master into the breed. This cross was successful, but it cost the breed some of its working ability.

In addition, the Bagusts admired the working ability of the Black and Tan Kelpie, a breed in development itself at the time, and added this blood to the Blue and Red Heelers. This final infusion set the breed type, gave the blue dogs their distinguishable tan "points," gave the red dogs deep red markings instead of black and was the direct forebear of today's Australian Cattle Dog.

The breeders of the day included Jack and Harry Bagust, Alex Davis (the son of Fred) and Robert Kaleski. These men continued the breeding of Queensland Heelers or Queensland Blue Heelers, keeping only the pups that were closest to the ideal. In 1902 Robert Kaleski drew up the first breed standard for the Cattle Dog. He based his standard on the Dingo type, believing that this was the ideal to strive for in the conditions of the country in which it was developed. The breed became known as the Australian Heeler and, eventually, as the Australian Cattle Dog. Robert Kaleski continued to preserve, write about and champion the breed until his death in 1961.

THE MCNIVEN DOGS

In the 1940s, Dr. Allan McNiven, an Australian veterinarian, decided to infuse Dingo blood back into the Australian Cattle Dog, as he felt that the breed was getting soft in both temperament and body. McNiven's dogs were imported heavily by ranchers in the United States for work with cattle and other livestock. When the Royal Agricultural Society Kennel Council (R.A.S.K.C.) discovered that Dr. McNiven was crossing purebreds with the Dingo, they banned him from showing and all his dogs were removed from the registry.

The Australian Cattle Dog in the U.S.

In the late 1960s, two Australian Cattle Dog owners, Esther Ekman and Christina Smith-Risk, sat ringside at a California dog show and discussed their love for the breed. Talk turned to forming a parent club for the

The Australian Cattle Dog became an AKC recognized breed in 1980.

breed in the United States with the express purpose of drawing up a breed standard and moving the Australian Cattle Dog out of the AKC's Miscellaneous Group. As it takes at least two members to form a club, the Australian Cattle Dog Club of America (first named "The Queensland Heeler Club of America") was born. Chris and Esther set out to find other like-minded fans of the breed, and in two years' time they had a total of twelve members or families interested in pursuing the recognition of the Australian Cattle Dog by the AKC.

The AKC explained to this group that all dogs entered into their studbooks must be traced directly back to those dogs registered in Australia. As the potential founding members started their extensive research, they discovered that many of their dogs were not actually traceable to the registered dogs in Australia. At this point, the members faced a painful decision, as most of the dogs they had could not be entered into the AKC studbooks as purebred Australian Cattle Dogs. Putting their love for the breed and their desire to do justice to its purebred heritage before their own personal investments, they took a firm stand that all dogs accepted into this initial registry must be traceable, on paper, to their Australian roots. This meant

that many of the dogs that were in the U.S. as "Australian Heelers" or "Queensland Heelers" were seen as not truly purebred because many of their ancestries could be traced to McNiven's dogs or other suspected crosses.

The AKC took over the breed registry in 1979 and the Australian Cattle Dog was fully recognized in 1980.

Since the decision in the 1960s to use the AKC as the true keeper of the Australian Cattle Dog studbooks, several other registry bodies in the United States have registered the breed. Registries other than the AKC, however, do not require any sort of documentation to prove that these "heelers" are traceable to purebred roots. Many sprang from McNiven's dogs or other crosses and cannot be guaranteed to be truly pure Australian Cattle Dogs. Such a dog can be registered with the American Kennel Club under its Indefinite Listing Privilege (ILP) program as long as he or she is neutered or spayed. See chapter 13 for more information about the AKC and other registries.

The Australian Cattle Dog Club of America (ACDCA) is still a vital force in the promotion and protection of the breed. Membership is open to anyone with a love for or interest in Australian Cattle Dogs. The ACDCA sponsors yearly National Specialties, in which a week of activities highlights the versatility of this marvelous breed. For more information about the ACDCA, see the addresses in the resource section of chapter 3.

The Australian Cattle Dog Today

The versatility and intelligence of the Australian Cattle Dog are quite remarkable. They are capable of performing many different jobs with and for their human companions. The Australian Cattle Dog's trainability, intelligence and problem-solving skills, coupled with her medium-size build, overall health and easy-to-care-for coat, make her a delightful companion.

WORKING FOR A LIVING

Many Australian Cattle Dogs continue to do the work for which they were bred. The breed's versatility makes them excellent workers on the wide-open range and on the small family farm. They can handle all kinds of livestock, from wild cattle to sheep and goats to pigs. Those involved in the cattle industry use Australian Cattle Dogs daily in any situation where the livestock is moved from place to place. This breed is often the top choice for working in feed lots and sale yards. The Australian Cattle Dog has the tenacity and force necessary for loading even the most stubborn cattle into transport trailers. In work environments where thousands of pounds of beef on the hoof must be loaded through chutes, gates, narrow corridors and aisleways, the Australian Cattle Dog is worth more than several extra pairs of hands. Many a tale has been told of an Australian Cattle Dog saving the life of her owner by keeping an ornery steer at bay long enough for her master to get out of harm's way in these close working situations.

FAMOUS OWNERS OF AUSTRALIAN CATTLE DOGS:

George Strait

Picabo Street

Mel Gibson

Gary Wilkes

Kelly McGillis

The Australian Cattle Dog excels at driving livestock from place-to-place and has the energy and stamina to assist a lone rancher in doing the work of many men. This breed is agile and tough enough to get into the brush to work stock out into the open where men on horseback or all-terrain vehicles can move them back into the herd.

On the small family farm, Australian Cattle Dogs are used as assistants for numerous jobs. With control and training, the Australian Cattle Dog can be used on all types of livestock. This breed is ideal for moving stock from pasture to pasture or into and out of the barn for the day. Milking, shearing and other daily chores can all be made easier with the assistance of an Australian Cattle Dog.

It is recommended that the Australian Cattle Dog NOT be left out as a stock guardian as her tendency is to work. Livestock left out alone with an Australian Cattle Dog will undoubtedly be worked around the pasture all day long. The Australian Cattle Dog must also be watched carefully around horses as the breed's propensity to heel things will certainly get her in trouble. The well-aimed kick of a horse can mean the quick demise of even an Australian Cattle Dog that is very well trained on other types of livestock.

GAMES COWDOGS PLAY

When the Australian Cattle Dog was admitted to the American Kennel Club in 1980, she became fully eligible for participation in AKC-sponsored activities and competitions such as herding, obedience, agility and tracking. I have outlined some of the more popular ways to spend time with your Australian Cattle Dog below; see Chapter 9, "Getting Active with Your Dog," for more information about things that you and your dog can do together.

The Australian Cattle Dog's breeding history as a herding dog also makes her a great contender in many AKC events.

CONFORMATION

This is the event that most people think of when they hear the term "dog show." This part of canine competition allows breeders to have their dogs evaluated against the breed standard (see chapter 1) in competition with other Australian Cattle Dogs. In these shows, Australian Cattle Dogs compete against each other with the goal of attaining the title of "Breed Champion." Points given out by several different judges assure that the dog or bitch does indeed conform to the Australian Cattle Dog standard and is a decent specimen of the breed.

AGILITY

Agility is one of the fastest growing "dog sports" in this country, and people are finding that the Australian Cattle Dog athlete excels at this activity. Agility is a competition that uses both the brains and the brawn of the Australian Cattle Dog to the fullest extent. It is an obstacle course competition that pits an owner and dog against the clock as the team navigates jumps, weaves poles, teeter-totters, tunnels and boardwalks—and precision counts.

OBEDIENCE

The teamwork required for obedience competition is perfect for the loyal Australian Cattle Dog. However, the repetitive nature of the individual exercises sometimes gets too boring for the breed's ever-whirling mind, leading them to create their own fun in the obedience ring. Serious obedience aficionados who work with Australian Cattle Dogs must have a sense of humor and must not expect an unthinking teammate who will work like a robot.

HERDING

Aside from the dogs who earn their dinner by working livestock on a daily basis, there are also numerous types of herding trials and competitions. The American Kennel Club (AKC), All Herding Breeds Association (AHBA), the International Sheepdog Society (ISDS) and the Australian Shepherd Club of America (ASCA) are all groups that sponsor trials for all herding breeds that showcase the ability and instincts of our working dogs. These events attract dogs who work for a living, as well as herding dogs (and their owners) that just enjoy the thrill of the competition. There are even "weekend herders," whose suburban owners drive out to the country to training facilities or clinics in order to let their Australian Cattle Dogs experience herding and prove that their instinct is still true to their heritage.

FLYBALL

Flyball is another rapidly growing dog sport that almost seems to have been developed for the Australian Cattle

Dog. The breed's incredible athletic ability, willingness to please its owner, speed, stamina and love of tennis balls make them naturals for this competitive event. Flyball is a relay race that involves teams of four dogs that must race over hurdles away from their owners, retrieve a tennis ball from a special "flyball box" that pops the ball into the air, and then race back over the hurdles toward their owner and teammates. Australian Cattle Dogs excel at this type of activity and their humans can enjoy the teamwork and competition as well.

Members of the breed work superbly as assistance and rescue dogs.

SEARCH AND RESCUE

The agility, heartiness and stamina of the Australian Cattle Dog make the breed popular among those who voluntarily train for Search and Rescue. These teams search for lost people in the wilderness or in the aftermath of natural disaster. An Australian Cattle Dog was recently honored as a hero for her tireless work in the search for survivors of the Oklahoma City bombing.

THERAPY

Despite the Australian Cattle Dog's reserved nature around strangers, it makes an excellent therapy dog. Therapy dogs and their owners visit hospitals and nursing homes to bring love (in the form of a wagging tail) to those in need. Australian Cattle Dogs seem to have a gift for "reading" the emotions of those around them, making them excellent companions for this type of volunteer work. When my dog Cooper was injured in a herding accident, he had external pins holding his leg together for quite some time. This piqued the interest of a young girl with disabilities who lived nearby and they became fast friends. No matter how full of energy Cooper was, he always slowed down to half speed when he was around this young lady. It didn't take long before Cooper had convinced her that throwing a ball, an activity she had to work very hard to learn how to do, was a fun thing.

Assistance Dogs

Some family pets are now trained to assist their owners with everyday activities that many of us take for granted. Hearing dogs notify their hard-of-hearing owners of sounds that they should be aware of and guide dogs act as their masters' eyes. Assistance dogs help their disabled owners with retrieving dropped items, shutting off lights and other tasks that can help make independent living easier.

chapter 3

The World
According
to the Australian
Cattle Dog

The Australian Cattle Dog is, above all, a herding dog—a dog developed for his strong work ethic, tireless endurance and devotion to his owner. Choosing to live with an Australian Cattle Dog means choosing the instinctive characteristics that go along  with this breed. The herding instinct, especially in a "heeling" breed, is strongly ingrained in the character of the breed.

A Social Dog

The Australian Cattle Dog is a very social breed with a distinct need to be part of the activity of the household. The breed does not take well to being separated from its human pack (family) for extended periods of time. The worst punishment you can inflict on a member of this breed is isolation from his "pack." An Australian Cattle Dog left out in the backyard quickly becomes bored and thus becomes a very destructive animal. An Australian Cattle Dog should never be tied or chained outside, as this will lead to frustration that will eventually grow into aggression.

Australian Cattle Dogs should also never be allowed to roam loose, even in rural settings. An Australian Cattle Dog left to his own devices will often find livestock to herd, and that trait can lead to dire consequences. In the country, many laws allow the immediate destruction of strange animals disturbing someone else's livestock. In the city, automobile tires (especially those that are moving rapidly) are often herding "targets" for the loose suburban cowdog.

The Australian Cattle Dog wants nothing more than to be your buddy, even when he is asked to accompany you in the most mundane chores or errands. Your dog will be thrilled to be included in a jaunt to the mailbox or a trip to take out the garbage. Cattle Dogs are often referred to as "shadow dogs" or "Velcro dogs" because wherever you go they are right behind you. Your Australian Cattle Dog will be happiest when allowed to be just under your feet or by your side.

The Australian Cattle Dog and Children

The Australian Cattle Dog is a devoted family companion, and this includes loyalty to the children of the family. As with any breed, supervision is necessary when the dog is around young children, until both learn how to interact with one another; ear and tail pulling by the toddlers should be discouraged, as should the dog's nipping. Socialization and obedience are key in keeping children and Australian Cattle Dogs happy together. The strength and exuberance of a playful Cattle Dog can easily knock down a young child. The high-pitched squeal of children at play will often set an Australian Cattle Dog into his protective mode. One must also remember that this breed has a keen eye for herding things that run by them rapidly. Children should be taught to be mindful of this trait, and simultaneously dogs should be trained to maintain control around children.

Australian Cattle Dogs are an intelligent breed that will constantly try to increase their status in your family "pack." Care must be taken to be sure that children maintain their status above the family dog. Remember that children are cherished members of the Australian Cattle Dog's pack, and these dogs will be protective of "their children," just as they are protective of "their home" and "their automobile." Be sure to watch your Australian Cattle Dog closely (especially during the dog's adolescent years) when children are roughhousing, as often this breed will perceive this sort of play as a threat. Dogs that cannot be controlled during this kind of activity should be removed from the area and should not be allowed to view the rough play from behind a window or a fence, as this will merely lead to built-up frustration.

With a little training, kids and Cattle Dogs will get along famously.

An Australian Cattle Dog will often use his herding instinct to "control" the human stock on his property. In yards where groups of children play, the Australian Cattle Dog will push them into a tight circle. There are many stories of Australian Cattle Dogs saving toddlers from running into traffic, or from straying away from the family property, by gently herding them back home.

Protective Instincts

The Australian Cattle Dog was bred to work by his master's side all day, and to protect the home and hearth all night. Anything that he considers to be his property will be guarded with suspicion. This often extends beyond the home to his owners, and even to the family automobile. Care should be taken to socialize a puppy early so that this protective instinct does not turn into aggression.

Even the most docile and sweet Australian Cattle Dog will surprise you with his protective instinct if he feels

Your dog will want to be wherever you are.

that your safety is in question. My very first Australian Cattle Dog, Hobart, was a sweet, gentle dog. Hobart often went jogging with a neighbor who did not have time for a dog of his own. One evening at dusk, Hobart and I were out practicing obedience in the park near our house. Without warning, he plastered himself to my right side and started to growl. This was the first time I had heard him growl and it took me by surprise. It happens that my neighbor was standing in the shadows watching us work and didn't want to disturb us. The moment that he stepped out into the light, where Hobart could recognize him, everything was fine, but I learned that day that, when suspicious, even the friendliest Australian Cattle Dog will ensure the safety of his owner.

Exercise

The Australian Cattle Dog is a high-energy breed, and needs an above-average amount of physical and mental exercise each and every day. Your Australian Cattle Dog will require two or more hours of *strenuous* exercise per day. If you cannot provide this sort of daily activity for your dog, think twice about becoming an owner. As mentioned previously, the Australian Cattle Dog is highly attuned to his owners and loves nothing better than to interact with them. Most Australian Cattle Dogs will not exercise if left alone in a yard or a run during the day. You must ensure that he gets his exercise in one way or another. Exercise can take the form of playing fetch with a ball or Frisbee, jogging, hiking, swimming or biking together.

The exhaustion of an Australian Cattle Dog's energy also requires keeping his mind active and challenged. His intelligence, coupled with his basic desire to work, *necessitates* obedience training. One of the most common questions about the breed is "Are they really that smart?" My answer is always the same, "Yes, too smart for the average human." Early obedience training classes, sometimes called "Puppy Kindergarten," can help continue the socialization that a good breeder begins (see chapter 8). Whether you take formal classes, work on household manners or teach your companion "parlor tricks," continuing obedience work with your dog as he grows and develops will only strengthen your bond as he works to please you. The more an Australian Cattle Dog learns, the more he wants to learn.

Working Instincts

The drive to work is intense in the Australian Cattle Dog. Fortunately for those "suburban cowdogs," work does not absolutely have to be herding livestock. The breed's desire to please can be channeled in many ways: patrolling the house, bringing in the morning newspaper, watching the children, even picking up his own toys or food dishes after dinner. There are also plenty of energy-burning "dog sports" in which Australian Cattle Dogs excel that can substitute for the work of their heritage.

Remember that the working instinct of the Australian Cattle Dog is what predisposes him to being a physically active dog, and requires him to be mentally challenged on a regular basis. Participating in some of the activities mentioned in chapter 2 will serve to form an incredible bond between man and dog, and it will also serve to keep an Australian Cattle Dog's mind active, occupied and healthy.

Choosing an Australian Cattle Dog

If you have adopted an Australian Cattle Dog out of serendipity then your choice was made for you. If you are searching for an Australian Cattle Dog, there are several avenues that are best for finding one that is healthy and well socialized.

BREEDERS

Find a breeder who knows and cares about the breed's instincts and heritage. Responsible breeders will have their dogs tested regularly for the genetic disorders prevalent in the breed, and will be able to tell you about these anomalies (see chapter 7). Beware of any breeder who does not know about the genetic disorders seen in this breed or who denies the existence of such problems. Unfortunately, the Australian Cattle Dog's genetic disorders are not simple problems that

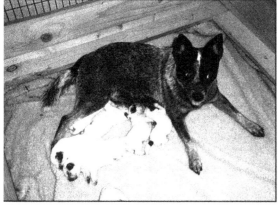

Most breeders will help you choose your dog from a litter.

can be helped with a daily pill or special treatment. Blindness, hip dysplasia and deafness can crop up without warning, so dogs must be thoroughly screened for these diseases before breeding (see chapter 7 for a complete discussion of these health problems). Most responsible breeders will help you choose your puppy from a litter. Remember that this breeder has spent at least eight weeks with these puppies and knows their personalities very well. If you have the opportunity to choose from the litter, it is wise to choose neither the boldest puppy nor the most timid. With Australian Cattle Dogs, the middle-of-the-road puppy is your best bet, as most inexperienced people will not be able to handle the truly overly outgoing Australian Cattle Dog.

BREED CLUB RESCUE

Breed Club Rescue is another way to obtain an Australian Cattle Dog. There are many reasons that members of the breed are rescued. Some are found in shelters as strays, and others were surrendered by owners who were unable to care for them for one reason or another. Some of these special Australian Cattle Dogs carry baggage from an abusive or neglectful past, while others are the most delightful companions. These dogs are often placed in temporary foster homes in which an experienced Australian Cattle Dog fancier can assess personality and temperament. These foster families can work with you and help you decide if a certain dog will suit your needs and fit into your household. While many of these dogs are older, breed rescue does occasionally have puppies available. Choosing to bring a rescued dog into your life can be extremely rewarding for both you and your new companion. Please see the resources section at the end of this chapter for contact information for The Australian Cattle Dog Club of America Breed Rescue program.

Cattle Dogs love snow—but be careful! Like humans, they are subject to frostbite.

Living with an Australian Cattle Dog
Climate

The Australian Cattle Dog is a hearty, healthy breed that can adapt to both cold and warm climates. Despite his development as a dog that can tolerate the heat of the outback, the Australian Cattle Dog adores the cold and snow. His doublecoat grows plush and thick in the winter months and protects him from the cold. You must be cautious playing with Australian Cattle Dogs in the snow because they will not give you any indication that it's time to go inside. Just like our exposed flesh, their paws are subject to frostbite and must be watched carefully.

BARKING

By reading the breed standard some people get the idea that the Australian Cattle Dog is a quiet breed. The working Australian Cattle Dog, intent on what he is doing, is generally a silent worker. An overly eager worker, a young or inexperienced dog or an Australian Cattle Dog faced with recalcitrant livestock may

The properly trained dog will not only get along with other breeds, but other types of animals as well.

occasionally use his voice, but this is the exception rather than the rule.

Under everyday circumstances, however, the Australian Cattle Dog is not a quiet dog. Like most canines, this breed vocalizes in order to express its emotions. The Australian Cattle Dog will yip and even moan, groan or yodel when playing. Many Australian Cattle Dog owners find that their dog has an exceptionally high-pitched, shrill and screeching bark that can be incredibly offensive. Keep in mind that the Australian Cattle Dog is highly protective of his property. This protective instinct often leads to repeated warning barks from Australian Cattle Dogs in response to noises or distractions that might not even merit the attention of other breeds. If left alone and bored, they will let you know that they are displeased by barking repeatedly.

OTHER ANIMALS

The properly socialized Australian Cattle Dog will get along with any other dog of any breed he meets.

However, some breeds are a bit put off by the Australian Cattle Dog's style of play. Romping Cattle Dogs often will herd their playmates by nipping them in the hocks, the same way they would herd livestock. Initially, other breeds will not understand that this is play and will take the nipping as an affront. It generally does not take long, however, for the "nipper" and the "nippee" to form fast friendships.

The Australian Cattle Dog must be exposed to cats and other small pets (rabbits, ferrets, etc.) either very early or very carefully, or these small creatures will be seen as prey. The Australian Cattle Dog has an exceptionally high prey drive. While it is this instinct that makes them an incredible herding breed, it is also the cause for concern around smaller animals. Care should always be taken with the Australian Cattle Dog around an animal that he might, under any circumstance, consider to be "fair game" to chase or herd. An over-exuberant Australian Cattle Dog, even one with obedience training and titles, should always be watched carefully in circumstances where instinct may take over training.

NIPPING

One must always remember that the Australian Cattle Dog was bred to nip at the heels of livestock. This is a deeply ingrained instinctual behavior that is part of the breed's genetic makeup. This is not a trait to be taken lightly or to be left unchecked. The Australian Cattle Dog's nip will rarely break skin, but it will leave a good bruise if contact is made. The Australian Cattle Dog constantly uses his mouth in play, snapping at the air and at toys. Any nipping, mouthing or biting directed at people should be discouraged as soon as it starts.

Puppies should remain with their litter until they are at least eight weeks old. During the sixth and seventh weeks of life they learn from their littermates and their dam (mother) that nipping hurts when you are on the receiving end. Persistence and training are essential if your Australian Cattle Dog did not learn bite inhibition as a young puppy. Bite inhibition can be taught in several different ways, but the best is to take the dog, either a puppy or older dog, "back to his youth" and act either like his dam or one of his littermates.

The first method to try out in this situation is to cry and whine like a puppy when your dog nips at you. Pretend that you are *really* hurt and leave the area of play whining loudly. Your Australian Cattle Dog will certainly follow you and want to resume play. Continue playing until any type of mouthing happens again and go through the routine of crying and leaving once again. Your Australian Cattle Dog will quickly learn that if he wants to play, he cannot use his mouth.

If your Australian Cattle Dog persists in nipping or mouthing in play, you must employ other methods to stop the behavior. While these dogs do not respond well to physical force, a firm hand and display of your dominant status in the pack are sometimes necessary. When your Australian Cattle Dog nips, firmly grab his muzzle with one hand and growl "no bite" in a deep guttural voice. Look directly into his eyes and wait until he submits and looks away. If he continues to challenge you by nipping, seek the help of a behaviorist or an obedience trainer as soon as possible.

THE HAIR OF THE DOG

The Australian Cattle Dog does not constantly shed his coat, but he blows out all of his undercoat once or twice a year. This is covered in detail in Chapter 6, "Grooming Your Australian Cattle Dog."

A Great Friend

With proper socialization and a lot of time and training, the Australian Cattle Dog can become the most wonderful companion you will ever have the honor of living with. There are many people who have great difficulty surviving the first few years of their Australian Cattle Dog's life, and then fall in love with the breed. Persistence, love, exercise and training are the vital tools for living with an adolescent Australian Cattle Dog.

One of the best mottoes for people living with this breed is: "A tired Australian Cattle Dog is a *good* Australian Cattle Dog!"

More Information on Australian Cattle Dogs

NATIONAL BREED CLUB

The Australian Cattle Dog Club of America
Katherine Buetow—Secretary
2003B Melrose Drive
Champaign, IL 61820

Amy Berry—Breed Rescue Chair
62022 Belmont
Joshua Tree, CA 92252

THE WORLD WIDE WEB

http://www.cattledog.com/

http://www.cattledog.com/acdca.html

BOOKS

Edwards, Cheryl. *Australian Cattle Dogs, Old Timers*. Sydney, Australia: YFP Publications, 1995.

Harling, Donn and Deborah. *Australian Cattle Dogs: The First Five Years*. Parsons, Kansas: Sun Graphics, Inc., 1986.

Holland, Virgil S. *Herding Dogs: Progressive Training*. New York: Howell Book House, 1994.

Holmes, John. *The Complete Australian Cattle Dog*. New York: Howell Book House, 1993.

Redhead, Connie. *The Good Looking Australian, The Australian Cattle Dog*. Adelaide, Australia: Lutheran Publishing House, 1979.

VIDEOS

The Australian Cattle Dog, American Kennel Club.

Living
with an

part two

Australian Cattle Dog

chapter 4

Bringing Your
Australian
Cattle Dog
Home

If you have decided to bring an Australian Cattle Dog into your life, either as a puppy or an older dog, there are certain supplies you will want to have on hand to make the transition smooth.

Collar and Leash

While this choice often boils down to personal preference, the best type of collar to intially put your Australian Cattle Dog in is one that buckles; these come in leather or nylon and can have a standard buckle or a quick-release plastic closure. With a rapidly growing puppy, you are best off getting an adjustable collar that can be easily resized as your puppy's neck expands. Be sure that the puppy is not able to slip out of the collar by backing out of it while on lead. With the breed's broad skull, however, this is not a common problem.

When you begin obedience training, your instructor may introduce you to several other types of collars or head halters that can be invaluable tools when working with the strong and energetic Australian Cattle Dog.

There is a wide variety of leashes for you to choose from to control your dog outside of a fenced yard. The 6-foot nylon or leather lead is standard, but retractable leads are popular when lead-breaking your puppy and when walking in wide-open spaces.

Identification

Your Australian Cattle Dog should wear identification on her collar at all times. This identification should include your name and phone number. If you travel frequently, you can get identification tags that are small round tubes in which you seal a piece of paper containing contact information. The information in these tags can be easily changed to reflect your current location.

A collar, leash and identification tag are necessary for your dog's safety.

PERMANENT IDENTIFICATION

Permanent identification is also becoming quite popular. Because dogs that get lost often lose their collar and tags, tattooing and microchipping are becoming commonplace. Ask your veterinarian about both of these alternatives.

Food and Water Dishes

There is a variety of dog bowls that will suit your needs. Some people like plastic, others like ceramic or stainless steel. Regardless of your choice, be sure that the food bowl is easily cleaned and will hold 6 to 8 cups. You should be a bit more careful in your choice of a water bowl for your pet, as Cattle Dogs have a tendency to play and splash in water. Be sure that the bowl you choose is unspillable and able to hold 2 to 3 gallons of water. If your dog decides that water is fun to play in, you may choose to keep the bowl outside, or on a mat that will absorb any spills.

Chow down!

Food

Discuss with your breeder what type of food your puppy is currently being fed, and ask for advice on when to switch to adult food (see chapter 5). Regardless of whether you are bringing home a puppy or adopting an adult dog, be sure to obtain a small amount of the food that the breeder is currently feeding her. Because extreme, rapid diet changes will often lead to an upset stomach and diarrhea, when switching the brand or type of food, begin the transition by mixing the old type of food with the new type. While

Australian Cattle Dogs are known for their ability to eat anything put before them, don't take this trait for granted. See chapter 5 for a more complete discussion of food and nutrition.

Crate

Your new Australian Cattle Dog will require a crate (kennel) to serve as a bed and a quiet place to call her own. The crate can be an invaluable tool for housebreaking a new puppy, as dogs will not soil their own "dens." The crate can also act as a restraint in the car to keep your dog safe in the case of an accident. This crate can be the molded plastic airline-style crate or a heavy, metal wire cage. Your choice depends on your preference and what your dog feels comfortable in. Whichever style of crate you decide to use, be sure to get one that will accommodate your Australian Cattle Dog when she is fully grown.

Toys

If you are bringing home a puppy, you will soon experience the joys of teething and, consequently, of an Australian Cattle Dog who will need an outlet for her chewing. Dogs are individual in their chewing likes and dislikes. Some prefer rawhide (cured beef hide), others prefer hard rubber and floss-style–rope toys. These types of toys provide relief for the teething puppy and are safe for her to chew on while she is unsupervised or in her crate. With the active Australian Cattle Dog puppy you need to watch stuffed toys or soft plastic toys (especially those with squeakers), as small pieces of latex or large hunks of stuffing can quickly become lodged in a puppy's throat or cause intestinal blockage.

A teething dog will need a reasonably sized piece of rawhide.

43

The older Australian Cattle Dog is just as tough on her toys as when she was a puppy. Tennis balls, Frisbees and indestructible balls are favorites of both Australian Cattle Dogs and their owners. Most Australian Cattle Dogs will persist in playing fetch with a Frisbee or ball until you tire out (and you certainly will tire before she does!). Most Australian Cattle Dogs adore playing with large, heavy plastic balls that can be filled with sand or water. An Australian Cattle Dog will generally "herd" these balls for hours on end. Check with your local pet supply store for more ideas on tough toys that can withstand the Australian Cattle Dog's jaws.

Other Necessities

GROOMING TOOLS

Buying grooming tools is not as urgent as obtaining food and water supplies, but buying new things is part of the fun of bringing home a new addition to the family. For the basics, you will want nail clippers, a pin brush, a slicker brush and a comb. Grooming your Australian Cattle Dog with these tools is discussed in detail in chapter 6.

THE DOGGIE BED

Many people who are adding a new dog to their home are likely to want to purchase some sort of doggie bed. In all honesty, few Australian Cattle Dogs appreciate the comfort of those fancy padded beds found in most supply stores and catalogs. Australian Cattle Dog puppies occasionally like a fleece blankie to snuggle up with at night, but must be watched carefully so that they don't chew up the fabric or ingest their bedding.

Preparing Your Home

There are several things you will want to do around the house to prepare for your new arrival. It is recommended that you either bring your new dog home on a weekend or arrange to take several days off from work in order to facilitate the transition to your house and schedule.

WHERE TO PUT THE CRATE

First, place the crate somewhere in your bedroom near your bed. Dogs are den animals that want to be with their pack at all times. Setting the crate up next to the bed will give you eight hours during which the dog can hear you, smell you, see you and take comfort in your presence. If you are bringing home a puppy, this will also help you hear her if she whines or cries to go outside in the middle of the night. Get the pup used to her crate by making it a happy place for her to be, never using it as punishment. I recommend feeding the puppy in the crate to help her get used to it and see it as a special and positive place.

WHERE TO KEEP THE PUP

You must also decide where the puppy will spend her days. If you work in the home, this is less of a problem, as the puppy can be watched most of the time, and crated when careful supervision is not possible. If you work outside of the home, the puppy will be fine in her crate for short periods of time, but you will have to arrange to run home during the day for potty breaks.

If you are going to leave your Australian Cattle Dog outside during the day, make sure the run or yard is completely secure from a dog who may either attempt to dig under a fence or climb or jump over it. Make sure that the enclosure also prevents other dogs, coyotes or predators from getting in. Be careful to provide shade, shelter from the weather and a large, unspillable water bowl.

Puppyproofing Your Home

You will be amazed at the things that a bored or inquisitive Australian Cattle Dog, either a puppy or an adult, will find to get into. So, you must make sure that your home, garage and yard are free of things that can harm your new dog. The easiest way to approach this task is to see things from the dog's point of view—get down on your hands and knees and go through your house room by room. Look for anything that might look especially tempting to chew on, rip up or play tug-of-war with. Pay special attention to electrical cords, tissue boxes and items kept on coffee or end tables. Start paying attention to things left on the floor well within the puppy's reach—dirty clothes and shoes or slippers are especially tempting to dogs that like things with human scent.

Check the kitchen and garage for chemicals, cleaning supplies, small nuts and bolts or paint that is stored in low cabinets. Put childproof latches on doors that might be easily nosed open. Antifreeze is especially toxic to dogs, but is unfortunately pleasing to their taste buds, so be certain that containers are well out of reach, and also make sure it isn't dripping on the garage floor or driveway.

Be sure that your dog won't be able to escape the confines of your yard.

In the yard, look for any way your Australian Cattle Dog might attempt to escape. Australian Cattle Dogs are incredible athletes; any fence that is less than 6 feet tall will possibly be too short to deter a dog with reason or desire to get out of the yard. Realize, of course, that sheer boredom is good enough reason for an Australian Cattle Dog to decide to leave the yard. Careful supervision is generally the only way to keep an agile Australian Cattle Dog inside a low-fenced yard. Be sure to look for places where a dog could possibly go over, under or through the fence. When you bring your new dog home, observe carefully whether she is actively looking for places to dig under the fence or loosen the boards. Repair any weak spots immediately.

Setting Up a Schedule

All dogs do best in a home where there is a relatively routine schedule. Regardless of the dog's age, a set routine is vital.

WHY YOU NEED TO HAVE A ROUTINE

Australian Cattle Dogs need plenty of exercise before extended periods of time during which they will be alone. Remember that puppies are just like any other baby—they sleep a lot and they need frequent potty breaks. As they grow older, puppies will sleep less and need more exercise and mental stimulation. A good rule of thumb is that a puppy can hold her bladder for about one hour per month of age. In other words, a three-month-old puppy will need to be let out every three hours, a five-month-old puppy every five hours, and so on. While this is often a tough thing to arrange with work schedules, you can often hire a pet sitting service to make several daily visits for you, or arrange for a neighbor to assist you.

WORKING OUT A SCHEDULE

Different homes have different schedules, but a sample routine for a young puppy might look like this:

6:00 a.m.   Puppy will be awake and ready to go out. Take puppy out to potty, praise puppy when she does her business. Come back inside and put puppy back in her crate.

7:00 a.m.   Get puppy back up again and take her out to potty, and again praise her when she does her business. Come back inside and feed the puppy. After she is done eating, take her back outside immediately and play, play and play some more.

47

Be sure to give her some quiet "cuddle" time before putting her back in the crate and going to work.

10:00 a.m. Arrange to have the young puppy taken out for a potty and play break with a pet sitter or a neighbor.

12:00 noon Come home from work and take puppy out to go potty, praise her when she does her business. Come back inside, feed puppy and have your own lunch. After she is done eating, take puppy back outside immediately and play, play, play, play, play. Give the puppy a kiss on the forehead, put her back in her crate and go back to work.

3:30 p.m. Arrange to have the young puppy taken out for a potty and play break with a pet sitter or a neighbor.

6:00 p.m. Get home from work and take puppy out to go potty, praise puppy when she does her business. Spend some time together doing basic training (see chapter 8) or playing. Put the pup back in her crate for a nap while you have your dinner.

8:00 p.m. Take puppy out to go potty, praise puppy when she does her business. Come back inside and feed. After she is done eating, take puppy back outside immediately and play again. Take this time to do your daily health care and grooming session (see chapters 6 & 7).

10:00 p.m. Take puppy out to go potty for the last time, praise puppy when she does her business. Bring puppy back inside and crate her for the evening.

Supervision

Even though you have taken the time to puppyproof your home, many behavioral problems can be circumvented early through careful supervision. Keep the young puppy under your watchful eye at all times while she is in the house. Use baby gates or other obstacles to keep the puppy in the same room as you or, if necessary, tether the puppy to you with a lead as you do household chores. Keeping an eye on a pup will speed housebreaking and keep her from chewing furniture and other inappropriate items. Keep a rawhide or chew hoof in your pocket, or within reach, in case the pup grabs for something that she shouldn't be chewing on. A simple "eh-eh-eh" or "phoey," while gently prying the inappropriate item from the puppy's jaws and replacing it with the appropriate chew toy, will get the point across very quickly.

Quality Time with Your Australian Cattle Dog

It cannot be emphasized enough that the Australian Cattle Dog will want and need your attention. Simply tossing your dog in the backyard for exercise will not suffice. The Australian Cattle Dog needs to be a "buddy dog." She needs both the physical companionship and the mental stimulation that she receives only by being with her human. Not all Australian Cattle Dogs will be crazy about tennis balls or Frisbees. It may take time with a pup or an adopted older dog to find a superior quality-time activity that really excites her, makes her eyes sparkle and brings the two of you closer together.

Crate Training

The dog's crate should not be considered a cage; it should be looked upon as the dog's "private space" or "den." Most dogs who are crate trained adore their crates and consider them happy places to be. Most dogs will go to their crates when they need a nap or some solitude—their crates are their retreat from obnoxious puppies or a nagging owner.

INTRODUCING YOUR DOG TO THE CRATE

Introduce your dog to the crate by transforming the effort from a chore into a fun game. Toss a biscuit or a toy into the crate and praise the puppy profusely when she enters. Never shove any dog into a crate against her will; if you do you will only make her fear it. Feeding your dog inside the crate will also help her become comfortable inside. One trick that can help calm anxiety in your absence is placing a worn T-shirt in the crate with the puppy. A puppy will naturally cry or whine when first crated overnight or as you leave for work. Remember that giving in and letting the puppy out of the crate because she is crying will simply reinforce the barking or whining and will lead to further behavioral problems.

CRATES DURING HOUSEBREAKING

There is no more valuable tool in housebreaking than a crate. A dog will not soil her den area. Taking a puppy out to potty and then crating her while she naps gives you some time to prepare yourself before she wakes with a full bladder and needs to go out again. Remember that a young puppy cannot hold her bladder for more than a few hours and so should not be left in the crate beyond that time.

A dog will make her crate her own personal space.

CRATES IN THE CAR

A crate is also a wonderful "safety belt" for a dog in a vehicle. Many dogs' lives have been saved because they were properly crated, even during minor traffic accidents. Crates will also help calm those dogs who get carsick or overly anxious on trips.

CRATES IN AN EMERGENCY

There is one last reason to consider crate training an Australian Cattle Dog. Sometime during her life, your Australian Cattle Dog will undoubtedly become sick or injured or need to spend time at the veterinarian's for some routine reason (like a spay or neuter). A dog in these circumstances will be overly stressed if she is not used to being crated even for short periods of time. Needless to say, this is a time when an Australian Cattle Dog needs all her energy to be focused on healing, and needless stress can be averted with just a little bit of early positive crate training.

chapter 5

Feeding
Your Australian Cattle Dog

Your Australian Cattle Dog will literally eat anything that you put in front of him. Very few are fussy eaters. Most have a voracious appetite that matches their appetite for life. It is up to you to make sure that the food your Australian Cattle Dog eats provides him with the nutrients his body needs during every stage of his life.

The Basic Building Blocks
PROTEINS

Proteins provide the body with amino acids that are essential for growth and cell repair. Amino acids are not synthesized by the body, and thus must be provided in the diet. A good commercial kibble company will use a high-quality protein source as the base for its food. Protein sources with high biological value include muscle meat, fish meal, eggs, milk and soybeans. The average dog requires a diet that is approximately 15 percent protein. Puppies will require about twice this amount for proper growth. Pregnant or lactating bitches, working dogs or exceptionally active dogs require approximately 20 percent protein in their diet.

FATS

Fats are a valuable energy source and provide your dog with linoleic acid, an essential fatty acid that is important for healthy skin and hair. Fats increase the palatability of food and also carry the fat-soluble vitamins D, E, A and K. Your Australian Cattle Dog will need different levels of fat in his diet throughout his life. A growing puppy needs around 15 percent fat in his diet. An active adult or working dog will need around 12 percent. The recommended level for the average adult is 10 percent.

CARBOHYDRATES

Sugars, starch and cellulose are all carbohydrates and are a valuable source of energy. Carbohydrates are found in grains, rice, potatoes and vegetables, and are most readily utilized when cooked. In order to allow for sufficient protein, fat and minerals in the diet, no more than 50 to 60 percent of a dog's ration should come from carbohydrates.

VITAMINS

Vitamins are essential elements necessary for the maintenance of health. Vitamins are classified as either water soluble or fat soluble. Water-soluble vitamins include the B complex vitamins, vitamin C, riboflavin, folic acid and biotin. Fat-soluble vitamins include A, D, E and K.

Vitamin B and B Complex Vitamins

Vitamin B and the B complex vitamins help to metabolize carbohydrates and amino acids. These vitamins also help protect the nervous system, assist in keeping the immune system strong and are vital in the maintenance of healthy skin and coat.

Vitamin A

Vitamin A is used by the dog's body to aid in fat absorption, and thus it is also necessary for the maintenance of healthy skin and coat. A deficiency of vitamin A will often cause problems with growth, reproduction and eyesight.

Vitamin D

Along with calcium and phosphorus, vitamin D is essential for the maintenance of healthy teeth, bones and muscles. An overabundance of vitamin D in the diet will lead to excessive mineralization of bone, tooth problems and possible calcification of the soft tissues. This example illustrates the potential hazards of over-supplementation.

Vitamin C

Vitamin C has been touted as a wonder vitamin for its immune system–boosting properties. Though some people feel that vitamin C supplementation can prevent hip dysplasia and boost the droopy ears of puppies, neither of these claims has been scientifically proven. However, since vitamin C is water soluble, any excess not used by the dog's body will pass safely in the urine.

Minerals

Like vitamins, minerals are essential elements in the health and well-being of your Australian Cattle Dog. Calcium and phosphorus are vital for the development of strong bones, teeth and muscles. Potassium is necessary for proper nerve functioning and, along with sodium chloride, helps maintain proper water balance. Iron and manganese both assist with metabolism, and zinc helps make up digestive enzymes and helps when tissue repair is needed.

Water

Water is of vital importance in the proper functioning of every living thing. Your Australian Cattle Dog needs water for proper digestion, nutrient transport, kidney function and waste removal. If possible, your dog should be given free access to clean, fresh water at all times. In hotter weather your dog will need more water, as he will be ridding his body of excess heat through evaporative panting. Dogs who have diarrhea should not be deprived of water, as dehydration can quickly lead to complications. If your dog exhibits excessive thirst, contact your veterinarian to rule out diabetes or kidney disorder.

Don't cage your puppy in with the wrong food!

Through the Years

The growing puppy, the adult dog and the canine senior citizen all have special dietary needs. During these three distinct phases of your Australian Cattle Dog's life you will need to adjust his diet in order to satisfy distinct nutritional requirements.

FEEDING THE AUSTRALIAN CATTLE DOG PUPPY

Puppies require about 50 percent more calories per pound of body weight than adult dogs, and approximately twice the protein. These special nutritional requirements should be continued until a puppy is six to eight months of age. Extra protein and fat are found in most commercially available puppy foods. The average puppy's daily needs are approximately 100 calories for every pound that he weighs. This figure will vary, as individual dogs have different metabolic rates. The product documentation for your food of choice will have nutritional information that can help you decide exactly how much food your puppy needs.

Supplementation of a puppy's diet should not be necessary and doing so could possibly cause more harm than good. You should be careful not to let an Australian Cattle Dog puppy stay "roly-poly" beyond about two months of age. While this may look cute, the added weight is extremely unhealthy for proper bone and muscle growth. It has been proven that hip dysplasia is linked to environmental factors, one of which is extra weight being carried during the first two years of growth.

FEEDING THE ADULT AUSTRALIAN CATTLE DOG

As your puppy reaches adulthood his nutritional needs will change. Between the ages of six and eight months you should switch him over to a lower protein, lower fat diet. As your Australian Cattle Dog reaches adolescence and enters adulthood, he will only need about thirty calories per pound of body weight. This figure will vary greatly depending on your dog's activity level. The best way to gauge the amount that your dog needs to be fed is to work with the recommendations made by the manufacturer of the food that you choose, and vary them slightly as necessary. Working or high-performance dogs will need extra calories and more frequent feedings to avoid hypoglycemia.

FEEDING THE AGING AUSTRALIAN CATTLE DOG

The aging Australian Cattle Dog will eventually slow down and need a diet that is lower in fat and higher in fiber than when he was younger and more active. It may seem that your Australian Cattle Dog's activity level will never subside, and most are very boisterous and active well beyond the age of ten, but their metabolism at this age is not what it was as a younger dog. Obesity is one of the leading causes of health problems in the aging canine, so weight should be monitored closely. You should not be able to see your Australian Cattle Dog's ribs, but you should be able to feel them as you run your hands down his side.

An older dog may also experience difficulty with nutrient absorption and may require vitamin or mineral supplements. If your older Australian Cattle Dog is not thriving the way he used to, it might be noticeable in a dull expression or a lackluster coat. Discuss these concerns with your veterinarian. He or she might suggest that you add a daily liquid or chewable vitamin supplement to your dog's diet.

Soup's on!

Choosing What to Feed

As advised in chapter 4, start by feeding your puppy or older dog what he was being fed before he came into your home. If you decide to change the brand of kibble that you are feeding him, do so gradually. Commercially available foods must all meet NRC (National Research Council) nutritional requirements, but not all of them will allow your Australian Cattle Dog to thrive. Ask your breeder or your veterinarian for advice on what brand of food to use. Then, using the information included in this chapter, look at the product literature and make an informed decision on what brand to use. In general, the adage "you get what you pay for" applies well to commercial dog food. Cheaper brands will use lots of fillers and high concentrations of carbohydrates, both of which will lead to loose stools and well-less-than-optimal nutrition. Overall, you are always best off paying for a better quality, more expensive food.

HOMEMADE DIETS

Some people choose to take the time to prepare food for their Australian Cattle Dogs. If you decide to do this, research the subject thoroughly in order to ensure that your dog is getting the nutrition that he needs. There are numerous books on the subject, and veterinarians who specialize in canine nutrition can be consulted to ensure that you are providing the proper balanced diet for your dog.

DRY OR CANNED?

Given a choice, most dogs will choose canned food over dry because it's higher in fat, moisture and meat content. Most owners, on the other hand, choose to feed dry food for its higher nutritional value per pound of food and lower price. Dry food has the added advantage of keeping tartar from building up on teeth as it naturally scrapes the teeth and gums when the dog chews his meal. Many people choose to feed a diet that is primarily dry kibble with the occasional spoon of canned food mixed in for variety. The addition of canned food is also helpful when feeding finicky eaters, older dogs or puppies that need additional fat in their diet.

Feeding Your Australian Cattle Dog
HOW MUCH?

The amount of food that you should allot to your Australian Cattle Dog varies depending on the dog's individual metabolism, the kind of food, the time of year and the dog's current activity level or special needs. Read the nutritional information on the food package. Watch your dog's weight carefully, and adjust the amount of food he is eating accordingly.

How Often?

A growing puppy needs to be fed three to four times a day. The adult dog can be fed once or twice per day depending on personal preference. Most dogs do best with their daily ration split between two meals served about twelve hours apart. Timed feedings help you set the schedule in your home, make housebreaking easier and remind him that you are the pack leader.

Supplements

As mentioned previously, there are rare special conditions and times in your Australian Cattle Dog's life when you will want or need to supplement his diet with extra vitamins, minerals or fatty acids. Consult your veterinarian or a canine nutritionist if you feel that you may need to add anything to your dog's diet, and remember that supplementation can often do more harm than good.

Treats and Snacks

The occasional biscuit or bedtime treat will not ruin an Australian Cattle Dog's appetite, but care should be taken not to overfeed him on snacks. Obesity will become a concern either in this instance or if the treats that you are using are too high in fat. Begging from the table or a mournful stare as you are cooking should never be rewarded. If you use food in training, consider using your dog's regular kibble as a treat and saving other treats as very special rewards for excellence. If you do offer your dog treats, be sure they are specially formulated for his system and needs. You can also feed him natural treats such as carrots or apples.

Poisonous Foods

There are certain foods that should *never* be given to dogs under *any* circumstances. Both chocolate and onions need to be kept away from dogs completely. They contain chemicals that are extremely toxic to canines.

BONES

It is best not to give your Australian Cattle Dog any bones. Certain beef bones are relatively safe, but others are not. Poultry and pork chop bones can shatter into sharp-pointed pieces, and fish bones are as dangerous for dogs as they are for people.

chapter 6

Grooming
Your **Australian**
Cattle Dog

The Australian Cattle Dog is a wash-and-go breed. This does not mean that regular grooming is not necessary. Routine grooming sessions are vital for keeping your Australian Cattle Dog looking her best and will also help increase the bond you  have with your dog. Minor threats to a dog's health, such as lumps or cuts, are often found during a simple grooming session, and early detection can prevent the problem from becoming severe, as well as help to prevent future problems.

Coat Care

The Australian Cattle Dog has what is known as a double coat. The short, dense, wavy undercoat keeps the dog warm in winter and cool in summer. The coarser, straight outercoat works with the undercoat to protect the Australian Cattle Dog from all the elements.

Typically, the Australian Cattle Dog is not a heavy, constant shedder, but this doesn't mean that she doesn't lose hair on a regular basis. Australian Cattle Dogs tend to "blow their coat" once or twice per year depening on climate and gender (intact females tend to blow coat after each heat cycle). When an Australian Cattle Dog blows coat, she will lose most of her undercoat over a period of a week or two.

Give your dog a thorough brushing often.

BRUSHING

Under normal circumstances, the Australian Cattle Dog does not require any brushing at all. But, her coat will be healthier if you give her a good brushing once a week or so. If you start your Australian Cattle Dog with these simple brushing procedures when she is young, she will look forward to them later on. Most dogs love being brushed, combed and groomed, as it stimulates the hair follicles and is like an all-over body massage.

The Pin Brush

The best tool to use for weekly brushing is a pin brush. It looks like a normal hairbrush, with protective Teflon balls at the tips of each metal bristle. Use this brush over your Australian Cattle Dog's entire body. Always brush with the lay of the coat and pay attention to the feel of the brush as it glides over the coat, so you can further investigate any abnormal lumps or contours.

Blowing Coat

When your Australian Cattle Dog is blowing coat, you will want some specialized grooming tools to help you hurry the process. The more often you brush your dog when she is blowing coat, the quicker you can urge all of the undercoat out and the sooner the shedding stops. During the week or two that your dog is blowing coat, you may want to brush her as often as twice a day. You will be amazed at how much undercoat will come off of your Australian Cattle Dog. The short undercoat is densely packed in under the outercoat and will seem to pop out from everywhere when your dog starts blowing. A slicker brush has a flat, square head with multiple fine, bent teeth. Use this brush on her coat in both directions to loosen and gather the dead undercoat. You will probably have to clear off the tines of the slicker brush every few minutes during a heavy coat-blowing week. Be careful when using the slicker brush since it does not have protective ends and may scratch the dog's skin.

The Grooming Comb

Another useful tool when your dog is blowing coat is a simple metal grooming comb. It too will assist in loosening dead undercoat. The Australian Cattle Dog's coat is naturally resistant to, but not proofed against, gathering burrs and other extraneous items. When foreign objects manage to get into the hair, a metal comb will assist you in removing them.

Bathing

You will want to bathe your Australian Cattle Dog whenever there is a need. This need should be based on her living conditions and her daily activities. If your dog is a herding dog who sleeps on your bed, you may want to consider daily baths. If your Australian Cattle Dog is a therapy dog or in the public eye, you will want

*Early training
will help ensure
that your dog
enjoys bathing.*

her looking and smelling her very best at all times. Most Australian Cattle Dogs will find something smelly to jump into or roll in at every given opportunity, and should be bathed accordingly.

GETTING READY

Early positive training will make the bathing process a great deal easier and more pleasant when your dog is bigger and stronger. Be sure to prepare the bathing site and yourself before beginning the bath. Wearing old clothes is best, as you will most likely get wet. Have a dry towel, the shampoo you are going to use and a couple of cotton balls on hand. It is recommended that wherever you bathe your dog, you figure out a way to tether her. A lead affixed to a fencepost or a tub hand-grip will serve this purpose nicely. Be sure to test the temperature of the water that you will be using. If the water from a hose is too hot or too cold, it will be a very unpleasant experience.

NEVER USE SHAMPOO MADE FOR HUMANS

You should never use a human shampoo on your Australian Cattle Dog. The formulations for humans and canines are different because of natural pH differences in the skin. Check with your veterinarian or your breeder for recommendations on dog shampoos. Be sure to always follow the directions on the bottle, as many dog shampoos are packaged in concentrated form.

THE BATH

Brush your Australian Cattle Dog thoroughly to loosen dead hair before bathing. Put cotton balls in her ears to prevent water from getting into the ear canal. Proceed by getting her completely wet. Remember that the Australian Cattle Dog coat is specifically designed to resist water, so you may need to work a bit to get her soaked to the skin. Once the dog is entirely wet, work the shampoo into the coat thoroughly. Make sure you work up a good lather and follow the shampoo's directions carefully (many flea shampoos, for instance, must be left on for five minutes to be effective). Rinse all of the shampoo out of the dog's coat. Again, the weather resistance of the Australian Cattle Dog coat will be working against your efforts, so be sure to take extra time to rinse all of the soap away. In dry climates or during winter months you can use a coat conditioner to reduce static buildup. Using too much, however, will often change the weather-resistant property of the coat.

Before bathing, be sure to brush your dog's coat free of dead hair.

DRYING

Drying the Australian Cattle Dog beyond toweling her off is usually unnecessary. You need to take special care, however, with young puppies or older dogs who may not be able to thermoregulate well. With these dogs, or during winter months in cold climates, use a blow dryer or a hose on the outflow port of your vacuum cleaner to speed drying time.

Nail Trimmimg

If not approached in the proper manner, trimming your Australian Cattle Dog's toenails can be a monumental struggle. Introduce puppies to toenail trimming when they are very young and use plenty of treats to make this a pleasant experience. In order to keep them short, you must trim your Australian Cattle Dog's nails on a weekly basis. Failure to do this will lead to serious problems and hinder proper stance. It doesn't take very long for an unkempt foot to cripple a dog. Long nails are also prone to breaking or tearing, which can be particularly painful for your dog.

TRIMMERS

There are generally two types of canine toenail trimmers available for use. The first is a guillotine-type clipper; the second looks more like heavy-duty scissors with a rounded opening for the nail. Both designs are perfectly acceptable for use, but you might find a personal preference for one or the other.

BE CAREFUL!

The biggest challenge when learning how to trim a dog's nails is learning how far back to cut. Unfortunately, there is a small blood vessel, called the quick, which runs about halfway down the nail, and which needs to be avoided when trimming. Australian Cattle Dogs' toenails are particularly difficult to learn to trim because they have all-black nails, making the quick invisible. If you look at each nail carefully, you will see the hooked end of a toenail that is too long. Until you are comfortable that you know exactly where the quick is located, do not make one extreme clip. Instead, trim away a little bit of the hooked end of the nail at a time, being careful to avoid the quick.

If you do hit the quick, your dog may yelp and bleed a bit. Pet supply stores usually carry special styptic powder that you can keep on hand for such accidents. If you don't have this powder, ordinary flour or baking soda will suffice. Simply fill the bleeding nail with the powder to stop the bleeding. Another trick for stopping a bleeding toenail is to press the nail into an ordinary bar of soap.

NAIL GRINDING

An alternative to using nail clippers is using a hand-held grinder to slowly file your dog's nails. While it can be a challenge to teach a dog to get used to the sound of these electric or battery-powered tools, there are numerous advantages to a ground nail over a trimmed nail. Using either a stone or a sandpaper wheel, the dog's nail is slowly filed down. Grinding minimizes the chance of injuring the nail's quick and causing bleeding, and also leads to a smoother nail surface (an advantage that owners will notice more than the dogs).

Get the dog used to the "whir" of the nail grinder the same way you would introduce any new and potentially frightening stimulus. First, let the dog see and sniff the new tool without turning it on. Then, with the dog either on a grooming table or laying belly-up in your lap, start with short sessions of praising the dog, both verbally and with treats, while turning on the nail grinder. When the dog is comfortable with the sound of the grinder, gradually and gently touch it to the dog's toes. Remember that the vibration of the dog's toenails will be a very new sensation to her, so keep your sessions short and positive. If the dog gets too upset over any step, back up and reassure her that all is all right. Using this method, it won't take long for your Australian Cattle Dog to accept the use of a nail grinder.

Ear Care

The Australian Cattle Dog has an upright ear, providing good air circulation and thus lessening the chance of infection common to drop-eared dogs. Occasionally your dog may need her ears cleaned or need to have excessive wax buildup removed. Carefully use a square of gauze or a soft cloth wrapped around your fingertip. Dip the gauze in isopropyl alcohol, mineral oil or water and gently swab out the ear. You will most likely need to repeat this three to four times in order to fully clean the ear. If you notice your Australian Cattle Dog shaking her head or pawing at her ears, or if you notice discharge at the ear opening or an unpleasant odor, a trip to the veterinarian is on order.

Give your dog's ears a thorough cleaning as needed.

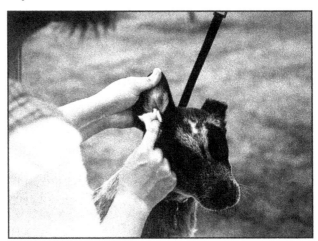

Eye Care

Your Australian Cattle Dog will occasionally get matter in the corner of her eye. This material is similar to the stuff that we have in the corner of our eyes when we wake up. If this happens, carefully use a damp tissue to wipe the matter out of her eye. If the problem persists, or if your dog's eye is red or swollen, consult your veterinarian immediately. He or she can prescribe an appropriate medication and regimen.

Dental Hygiene

While your puppy is still young, accustom her to having her mouth opened and her teeth and gums gently touched during grooming sessions. Checking your Australian Cattle Dog's teeth should be a part of your daily routine, but if needed, you should also clean them on a weekly basis. Some dogs seem to get tartar buildup more rapidly than others. Giving your dog rawhide or sterilized bones to chew, or feeding crunchy treats regularly, can usually keep tartar to a minimum.

Healthy teeth will be strong, sound and clean, and healthy gums will be firm and pink. There is no reason for a well-groomed dog to suffer from the effects of neglected oral hygiene.

The Tools of the Trade

There are several commercial specialized canine toothbrushes that will do a wonderful job of cleaning your dogs teeth. A soft human toothbrush and baking soda will also do nicely. You can make brushing a daily activity in order to avoid buildup altogether. A soft cloth or piece of gauze wrapped around your finger can wipe away food particles and the bacteria that lead to tartar. If buildup does occur, you can use a scraper similar to the tools that your dentist uses to remove tartar. Use this dental tool carefully, especially around the gumline.

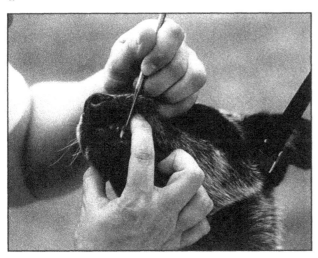

Use a scraper to remove plaque from your dog's teeth.

Bad Breath

Your Australian Cattle Dog's breath should not be extraordinarily bad. If your dog's breath has a foul odor, it may be an indication of an abscessed tooth or gum disease. Be sure to consult a veterinarian immediately if you notice a change in your dog's breath during your daily exam or weekly cleaning.

chapter 7

Keeping Your Australian Cattle Dog Healthy

The Australian Cattle Dog is generally an extremely hearty and healthy breed. *The Guinness Book of World Records* lists an Australian Cattle Dog named Bluey as the longest lived

dog in history. Bluey lived twenty-nine years and five months, and worked with both cattle and sheep for twenty of those years!

Our dogs rely upon us for routine medical care to keep them healthy and happy. You should make yourself as familiar as possible with the daily, monthly and yearly preventative and emergency care that will help keep your Australian Cattle Dog in good health his entire life.

Finding a Veterinarian

If you do not already have an established veterinarian, be sure to take the time to get recommendations from friends and visit the offices in your area before bringing your Australian Cattle Dog home. If possible, schedule an appointment to visit prospective veterinarians without your dog to get a general idea about their office procedures and their philosophies on both preventative and emergency care.

Try to find out whether the veterinarian you are considering is experienced with Australian Cattle Dogs. This is important in dealing with any breed-specific problems your dog may develop. Your dog's veterinarian should also be someone of whom you feel comfortable asking questions, someone who takes the time to explain things and lets you know how emergency or after-hours situations are handled by the office.

Daily Examinations

The Australian Cattle Dog is an extremely rough-and-tumble breed; they work hard, they play hard and they rarely show any sign of pain or injury. It is up to you to make sure that small injuries are caught early and don't turn into larger problems. To detect problems early, give your Australian Cattle Dog a good hands-on exam once a day. By making this a part of your daily routine, both you and your dog will come to enjoy it, and begin to see it as special bonding time.

Feel your dog daily to make sure he's free of lumps, parasites and other abnormalities.

Start at the dog's head and feel every inch of him. Foreign objects, ticks, fleas, mats or large scrapes or cuts will be readily apparent. Once you have become accustomed to the individual contours and idiosyncrasies of your Australian Cattle Dog's body, the smaller lumps and bumps will not escape your notice. Pay special attention to his feet and pads, looking for cuts, scrapes or burrs that may be stuck between his toes. Check his ears for foreign bodies and do a brief check of his teeth.

Unfortunately, dogs cannot tell us when they are feeling pain or illness. In fact, most Australian Cattle Dogs are so stoic they won't indicate to you that they are feeling bad. Most of us can tell, however, when our companion is just a little bit "off" for one reason or another. Before calling your veterinarian, you will want to assess the symptoms so that you can describe them to the best of your ability.

Assessing Health Problems

While we will include simple emergency-care procedures in the next section, you should never hesitate to call your veterinarian if you are worried about your Australian Cattle Dog's health. It is important to know all the details pertaining to your dog's illness, so that you can convey them to the vet. The following paragraphs contain some questions that you should ask yourself when assessing a health problem in your dog.

Regular veterinary checkups will help keep your dog in tip-top shape!

What exactly is wrong with your dog? Did you find an abnormal lump or painful area during your hands-on exam? Is he limping? Is he eating normally? Is he drinking normally? Is he urinating? Is his stool normal or loose? Is he vomiting? Ask yourself if your dog was in contact with any unusual things in the twenty-four to forty-eight hours prior to the examination, and if so, relay this information to your veterinarian.

DETECTING LUMPS AND SORES

If you have found a lump or sore, what exactly does it look like? Is it open or closed? Is the wound or lump hot to the touch?

DETECTING DIGESTIVE PROBLEMS

Run your hands regularly over your dog to feel for any injuries.

If your dog isn't eating, when was his last full meal? If he is vomiting, what does it look like and how often is it occurring? Is the dog drinking normally and urinating with regularity? Is there any blood in the urine? If your dog has diarrhea, is it exceptionally watery, mucus-filled or bloody? Are there any signs of intestinal parasites? (See the section on parasites, later in this chapter.)

DOES YOUR DOG HAVE A FEVER?

A dog's temperature should be taken rectally. Smear a bit of petroleum jelly on the end of a thermometer; insert and hold it in the dog's rectum for a full three minutes. A dog's normal body temperature is 101° to 102°.

IS YOUR DOG BREATHING NORMALLY?

The normal respiration rate should be ten to thirty breaths per minute at rest. It is a good idea to get a baseline for your own dog when he is not ill, so that you know what his normal range is.

WHAT IS YOUR DOG'S HEART RATE?

A dog's femoral arterial pulse is easily taken by feeling inside the upper rear thigh. Again, do this when your dog is in good health, so that you know what is common for your individual Australian Cattle Dog. The normal heart rate of a dog at rest is 70 to 160 beats per minute.

Emergency First Aid for Your Dog

The following are examples of instances in which first aid should be administered. Be aware that the procedures described here are not to be substituted for veterinary care, but to be used as a means of providing minimal aid in order to sustain your dog while you seek professional help.

THE EMERGENCY MUZZLE

A wounded dog, even a dog that would ordinarily never snap at a human, might bite out of fear or pain. The first step that should be taken when dealing with any injured dog is to muzzle him in some way. If you do not have a muzzle on hand, one can easily be made out of a leash, a scarf or a length of gauze. Wrap the material around the dog's muzzle and tie it once on top, then bring it back down under the muzzle and cross it under the jaw. Bring the makeshift muzzle back and tie it behind the dog's ears.

Use a scarf or old hose to make a temporary muzzle, as shown.

BLEEDING

If your dog is bleeding due to a cut or puncture wound, apply direct pressure to the site using a clean gauze pad. Clean the wound with hydrogen peroxide if possible. If you think the dog might need stitches, or if bleeding persists, call your veterinarian immediately.

ANIMAL BITES

If another dog or animal bites your Australian Cattle Dog, first stop the bleeding and then clean the wound with peroxide. If he is bitten by a dog that has not recently had a rabies vaccination, by a wild canine or by another animal (such as a skunk, bat, raccoon, squirrel, etc.) you will want to see your veterinarian as soon as possible. Keeping your dog's rabies vaccination up-to-date will mean less worry if he is bitten by a wild animal.

Snakebites

If a snake bites your dog, pay close attention to the patterns, colors and markings on the snake's skin. Then call your veterinarian immediately. Apply ice to the site to slow the spread of venom and get the dog to the veterinarian as quickly as possible. Do not allow the dog to walk or move around on its own if at all possible.

STINGS

Some of the many household substances harmful to your dog.

If a bee or wasp has stung your dog, apply ice to the site and call your veterinarian right away. Watch carefully for signs that your dog may be having an allergic reaction to the sting, which may cause swelling of the respiratory tract. If necessary, you can use an antihistamine to handle minor swelling. Consult your veterinarian for the proper dosage if this is necessary.

POISONING

Many products and plants can be toxic to your Australian Cattle Dog. Antifreeze is one such product, and unfortunately dogs are attracted to it because of its sweet taste. Insecticides, paints, household chemicals and various plants are all dangerous to curious dogs.

A number of houseplants, including avocado, dieffenbachia, English Ivy, jasmine, philodendron and the bulbs of the amaryllis, daffodil, hyacinth, narcissus, iris and tulip are poisonous. So are apple seeds, cherry pits, chocolate, mushrooms, peaches, rhubarb, tobacco and walnuts.

When your dog is outside, do not let him eat andromeda, arrowgrass, azalea, bittersweet, boxwood, buttercups, caladium, castor beans, choke-cherry, climbing lily, crown of thorns, daphne, delphinium, dieffenbachia, dumb cane, elephant ear, elderberry, foxglove, hemlock, hydrangea, laburnum, larkspur, laurel, locoweed, marigold, monkshood, nightshade, oleader, poison ivy, privet, rhododendron, snow on the mountain, stinging nettle, toadstools, wisteria or yew.

If you suspect that your dog has come into contact with or ingested any sort of poison, time is critical. *Do not induce vomiting until you are instructed to do so.* Indications of poisoning include vomiting, retching, drooling, labored breathing, weakness, collapse or convulsions. Call your veterinarian immediately. If you cannot get a hold of your veterinarian, call the National Animal Poison Control center at 1-800-548-2423.

HEAT STROKE

A dog that gets overheated may be in life-threatening trouble. If your dog is experiencing weakness or has collapsed due to the heat, get him into a tub of cold water immediately. If a tub is not available, run water from a hose over your dog to cool him off. Pay special attention to wetting the pads, ears and groin area, as these are the regions of greatest heat dissipation in a canine.

A FIRST-AID KIT

Keep a canine first-aid kit on hand for general care and emergencies. Check it periodically to make sure liquids haven't spilled or dried up, and replace medications and materials after they're used. Your kit should include:

Activated charcoal tablets

Adhesive tape
(1 and 2 inches wide)

Antibacterial ointment
(for skin and eyes)

Aspirin (buffered or enteric coated, *not* Ibuprofen)

Bandages: Gauze rolls (1 and 2 inches wide) and dressing pads

Cotton balls

Diarrhea medicine

Dosing syringe

Hydrogen peroxide (3%)

Petroleum jelly

Rectal thermometer

Rubber gloves

Rubbing alcohol

Scissors

Tourniquet

Towel

Tweezers

Encourage your dog to drink some cool water. Contact your veterinarian as soon as possible to avoid shock and secondary complications.

FRACTURES

Because a broken bone causes great pain, muzzle your Australian Cattle Dog and seek veterinary help immediately if you suspect he has this injury. Do not attempt to set the bone yourself, but if possible, immobilize it with a rolled-up magazine or newspaper and some gauze. If you can, use a board as a backboard or stretcher so that the injured limb stays stable. Transport the dog to the veterinarian as soon as possible.

Make a temporary splint by wrapping the leg in firm casing, then bandaging it.

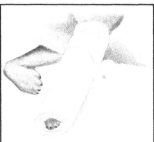

CHOKING

If your dog is pawing at his face, frantically panting or drooling, he may be choking. First, open the dog's mouth to see if you can see the obstruction. Often, a ball or a small piece of rawhide will be within reach. Be extremely careful not to push the obstruction further into the windpipe. If you cannot see an obstruction, but the dog is not able to breathe, you will have to execute a modified version of the Heimlich maneuver. With the dog lying on his side, press gently but firmly on the ribcage in an upward motion. You are trying to expel as much air from the lungs as possible in the hope of dislodging the obstruction with the

Applying abdominal thrusts can save a choking dog.

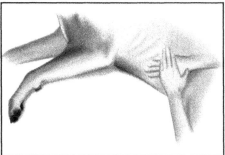

force of the air. Once you dislodge the object, see your veterinarian immediately to check for abrasions or lacerations in the windpipe.

Helping Your Dog Recover

There will be times in your dog's life when you will need to administer medication to your dog or take care of simple medical needs at home. Always follow your veterinarian's instructions, and always follow through completely on all courses of treatment.

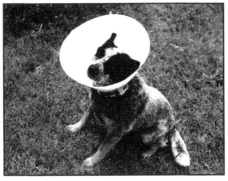

THE ELIZABETHAN COLLAR

If a dog has stitches, is persistently licking a wound or is constantly scratching his head, your veterinarian may recommend an Elizabethan

The Elizabethan collar.

collar. This large, plastic cone may look uncomfortable, and it definitely is clumsy and awkward for the dog, but it is often necessary to prevent the reopening or infection of a wound.

ORAL MEDICATIONS

Pills

There are several methods of giving a dog a pill. The easiest is to hide the pill in a bit of cheese or meat and give it to the dog. Be careful if you use this method, as many clever dogs will quickly learn how to eat the goodie and spit out the medication.

To give a pill, open the mouth wide, then drop it in the back of the throat.

If you need to manually give the dog a pill, stand behind him and open his mouth wide, with his muzzle pointing straight up. Drop the pill into the back of the throat and quickly shut the dog's mouth. Hold his mouth shut while massaging his throat until you see

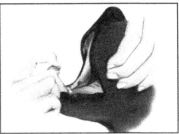

the dog swallow. Before you let him go, open his mouth and check to make sure the pill is gone.

Liquid Medication

Giving an Australian Cattle Dog liquid medication can prove to be a challenge. Some dogs will tolerate medication being poured directly into their mouths if care is taken to be sure that the liquid does not go down the windpipe. An easier way to give a dog liquid medicine is to use a large syringe or turkey baster to squirt the medication into the dog's mouth between his cheek and teeth. Do this while holding the dog's muzzle shut and his head tilted slightly backwards. His head should be tilted back slightly so that the medication will run into, instead of out of, the dog's mouth.

EYE OINTMENT

Squeeze eye ointment into the lower lid.

If you need to put ointment in a dog's eye, stand behind him with your legs on either side of his head. Make sure you give him a reassuring scratch or two under the chin before starting. Pull the bottom lid down with your thumb and squeeze a bit of ointment onto the lid. When the dog closes his eye, the ointment will be evenly distributed. Be very careful to pay close attention to the dog for a while, as his vision may be blurred initially due to the ointment.

SKIN OINTMENT

Applying skin ointment to an infected area is a simple task. Part the hair so that you're putting the ointment directly on the skin, and rub it in according to the directions. Keeping an Australian Cattle Dog from licking or rubbing it off, however, can be a formidable task. In many cases, licking or chewing any sort of wound will reduce healing time, or even cause secondary infection. One alternative is to spray a product that will taste bad on or near the wound. One product, Bitter Apple™, is commercially available for this use, but check with your veterinarian before using it near wounds, as its main ingredient is alcohol. Another alternative is the use of an Elizabethan collar.

Vaccinations and Infectious Diseases

The diseases listed below can be largely prevented in your Australian Cattle Dog by early and regular vaccination. Your dog should be vaccinated for all of the following diseases. Unfortunately, sometimes vaccines fail for one reason or another and fully inoculated dogs contract these diseases. It is of paramount importance to discuss a vaccination schedule with your veterinarian.

DISTEMPER

Canine distemper is a highly contagious airborne virus. Worldwide, canine distemper is the leading cause of infectious disease deaths in dogs. Distemper takes a variety of forms and often goes through several stages. Secondary infections and neurological complications are often a cause of death. In the first stage of canine distemper, dogs show signs typical of a human cold. Infected dogs will have a fever, become listless, have a watery discharge from the eyes and nose and will often lose their appetite. Within a few days, the discharge will change from watery to a thick, yellow and sticky mucus. Diarrhea often accompanies the infection and can lead to severe dehydration. After week one of the distemper infection, the dog may appear to get better and then worsen the very next day. The waxing and waning of symptoms in the second and third weeks of infection are typical of canine distemper. The second stage of canine distemper involves the brain. Dogs that show signs of this

YOUR PUPPY'S VACCINES
Vaccines are given to prevent your dog from getting an infectious disease like canine distemper or rabies. Vaccines are the ultimate preventive medicine: they're given before your dog ever gets the disease so as to protect him from the disease. That's why it is necessary for your dog to be vaccinated routinely. Puppy vaccines start at eight weeks of age for the five-in-one DHLPP vaccine and are given every three to four weeks until the puppy is sixteen months old. Your veterinarian will put your puppy on a proper schedule and will remind you when to bring in your dog for shots.

stage usually do not survive the illness. Signs of neurological involvement include head-shaking, drooling, turning in circles and ultimately, seizures.

Treatment for canine distemper is often unsuccessful unless caught extremely early. Antibiotics can be used to thwart secondary infection, but there is no known antibiotic that is effective against the distemper virus itself.

HEPATITIS

Infectious canine hepatitis is a highly infectious viral disease that should not be confused with hepatitis in humans. Canine hepatitis presents a wide variety of symptoms that can often be confused with canine distemper. This virus is shed in the saliva, stool and urine of infected dogs. In the acute form of canine hepatitis, symptoms include a fever accompanied by bloody diarrhea and vomiting of blood. Infected dogs will often protectively "tuck-up" their bellies, refuse to eat and show signs of jaundice due to liver dysfunction. Treatment of acute cases of infectious canine hepatitis involves hospitalization and treatment with large doses of B complex vitamins. In the fatal fulminating form of infectious canine hepatitis, the dog very rapidly becomes ill, develops bloody diarrhea, collapses and dies.

PARVOVIRUS

Parvovirus, or parvo as it is commonly known, is a highly contagious viral disease that causes inflammation of the bowel. The disease is usually acquired by ingesting the stool of infected dogs. Signs of this illness are evident three to ten days after exposure. Symptoms include fever, loss of appetite, depression, lethargy, vomiting and diarrhea (which may be bloody). The virus replicates quickly in many organs and spreads rapidly through the body. Dogs with the disease, especially young puppies, may die suddenly if the virus infects and weakens the heart. Treatment of parvovirus includes veterinary help to prevent the dehydration which results from vomiting and diarrhea. Antibiotics are used to prevent secondary complications due to bacterial infection.

CORONAVIRUS

Coronavirus is another viral bowel infection with symptoms similar to those of parvovirus. Coronavirus is often milder than parvovirus and is rarely fatal in adult dogs, but young puppies are still at risk of secondary complications. Treatment of this virus also includes fluid maintenance and antibiotic therapy.

Symptoms include vomiting, loss of appetite and a yellowish, watery stool that might contain mucus or blood. The stools carry the shed virus, which is highly contagious. Fluid or electrolyte therapy can alleviate the dehydration associated with the diarrhea, but there is no treatment for the virus itself.

LEPTOSPIROSIS

Canine leptospirosis is a disease caused by a bacteria called a spirochete. The disease is spread through the urine of an infected animal and enters a dog's system through a break in the skin or via the digestive tract. Indications of illness appear within five to fifteen days of infection and may

> ### WHEN TO CALL THE VET
>
> In any emergency situation, you should call your veterinarian immediately. You can make the difference in your dog's life by staying as calm as possible when you call and by giving the doctor or the assistant as much information as possible before you leave for the clinic. That way, the vet will be able to take immediate, specific action to remedy your dog's situation.
>
> Emergencies include acute abdominal pain, suspected poisoning, snakebite, burns, frostbite, shock, dehydration, abnormal vomiting or bleeding, and deep wounds. You are the best judge of your dog's health, as you live with and observe him every day. Don't hesitate to call your veterinarian if you suspect trouble.

be extremely mild. Fever is the first sign of infection, followed by loss of appetite, depression and general listlessness. While leptospirosis can affect many systems, the kidneys often show the first real signs of infection. The dog may display severe thirst and frequent urination. He will also guard his kidneys with a "hunched-up" gait. Vomiting and diarrhea follow the initial symptoms, along with sores in the mouth and blood in the stools. Treatment involves radical veterinary intervention and isolation of the dog. Great care should be used in handling the secretions of sick dogs as the spirochete can also cause disease in humans.

TRACHEOBRONCHITIS

Tracheobronchitis, commonly referred to as kennel cough, is a highly contagious respiratory disease caused by one of several viruses. A harsh, dry, spastic cough is the characteristic (and often the only symptom) of this disease. This airborne virus spreads rapidly within a kennel or home situation. Isolation of symptomatic dogs and quick treatment with antibiotics are critical in stopping the spread of this virus. The vaccine for this is administered through the nose (intranasally) by drops or a nasal spray.

RABIES

Rabies is a fatal disease that occurs in nearly all warm-blooded animals. Transmission of this virus is through the saliva of an infected animal, often by a bite. The virus travels initially to the brain and spinal cord. The incubation period for the virus is typically two to three weeks, but can take up to several months. The early signs and symptoms of rabies are products of encephalitis (swelling of the brain). The first signs of rabies infection are behavioral changes. Shy dogs may suddenly become outgoing and affectionate, or normally easy-going animals may become outwardly aggressive. As the virus spreads, minor neurological symptoms such as drooling, spinning or a head tilt may appear. The final stages of viral infection include seizures or paralysis. There is no treatment for an animal with rabies.

External Parasites
FLEAS

Fleas are small, bloodsucking insects capable of leaping incredible distances relative to their body size. While there are several species of fleas, none are host specific. Fleas are the intermediary hosts for tapeworms (see section on internal parasites, below) and are often the cause of allergic dermatitis. The discovery of a single flea on your Australian Cattle Dog is often a good sign that there are many more fleas nearby.

Fleas can be easily detected during the daily hands-on exam of your dog. While brushing your hand through the dog's coat, look for the small, scurrying flea trying to dart into the

The flea is a die-hard pest.

safety of the hair. Evidence of fleas can also be found by looking for their droppings, most often seen on the belly of the dog or near the genitals. You can also see fleas by having your dog lie on a solid colored sheet and brushing vigorously. if you see salt-and-pepper–type residue falling to the sheet, your Cattle Dog has fleas. The residue is made up of fecal matter (the "pepper") and the eggs (the "salt"). If your dog is suddenly scratching, it may be a sign of allergic dermatitis, which is an allergic reaction to the saliva of the flea.

Eliminating Fleas

Executing a thorough attack is the only way to eliminate fleas from your dog's immediate environment. Flea eggs can stay in a dormant state for literally years, awaiting the perfect hatch conditions. Not only must fleas be removed from the dog, but the entire environment must also be treated. Shampoos, dips and sprays can kill fleas on the dog. Bedding must be carefully washed in *hot* water and the house, yard and car must be bombed or sprayed to rid the area of adult fleas and eggs.

FIGHTING FLEAS

Remember, the fleas you see on your dog are only part of the problem—the smallest part! To rid your dog and home of fleas, you need to treat your dog *and* your home. Here's how:

• Identify where your pet(s) sleep. These are "hot spots."

• Clean your pets' bedding regularly by vacuuming and washing.

• Spray "hot spots" with a non-toxic, long-lasting flea larvicide.

• Treat outdoor "hot spots" with insecticide.

• Kill eggs on pets with a product containing insect growth regulators (IGRs).

• Kill fleas on pets per your veterinarian's recommendation.

If you have any questions about what is safe to use on your dog, call your veterinarian. If you have questions as to how to use a particular product, call the manufacturer, who will be more than willing to talk to you and explain exactly how the product should be used.

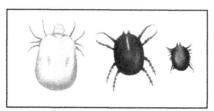

Three types of ticks (l-r): the wood tick, brown dog tick and deer tick.

TICKS

Ticks are another bloodsucking insect that can make both you and your Australian Cattle Dog miserable. Ticks can be found in grassy and wooded areas, and are known to carry numerous diseases including Rocky Mountain fever, Lyme disease and encephalitis. Ticks attached to a dog's skin and engorged with blood are especially easy to find when examining your dog. If one tick is found, do a very thorough exam of the dog to look for more.

Check for ticks when you examine your Australian Cattle Dog. Ticks seem to prefer to lodge in the ears or in the hair at the base of the ear, the armpits or around the genitals. The tick is slightly larger than a sesame seed when not engorged with blood.

Use tweezers to remove ticks from your dog.

Removing Ticks

Everyone has an individual method of removing ticks. The main thing to remember is that the entire tick must be removed from the dog. If the head of the tick is left burrowed in the skin, it may lead to infection and possibly abscess. Any person removing or touching the tick should use tweezers and surgical gloves. Smothering the tick is the best initial tactic. Smear petroleum jelly or drop alcohol on the tick and let it sit for a minute. Grasp the tick with tweezers and pull firmly to remove the entire head. Be sure to swab the area with disinfectant and check the site for infection over the next few days.

Internal Parasites

Internal parasites are commonly detected through a fecal sample by a veterinarian and should be treated under close supervision. The chemicals used to treat internal parasite infestations are toxic to their target, and thus are also potentially toxic to the dog if used incorrectly.

ROUNDWORMS (ASCARIDS)

Roundworms are most commonly found in the stool of puppies. They are small and threadlike in appearance, and they often look like white earthworms. Puppies are often born with this type of parasite, as the dormant roundworm is mobilized in the pregnant female and passes through the uterus to infect puppies.

Puppies with roundworm infestation often have a dull coat, a general failure to thrive and a "pot-bellied" appearance. Roundworms are transmitted by eggs that are shed in an infected dog's stool. Because of this mode of transmission, care should be taken to pick up your yard daily, and dogs should be discouraged from investigating any other dog's stools in any way.

Common internal parasites (l-r): roundworm, whipworm, tapeworm and hookworm.

If treated early, roundworms are not serious. A heavy infestation, however, can seriously affect a dog's health.

TAPEWORMS

Tapeworms are most commonly transmitted to a dog by their intermediate host, the flea. They can also be transmitted when a dog consumes infected raw meat (or prey) or fish. Tapeworm segments can be detected in the stool and often look like little grains of rice. Tapeworms often cause gastrointestinal upset, general malaise, diarrhea and possible loss of appetite. Flea control is of utmost importance in taking care of the cycle of tapeworm infestation.

WHIPWORMS

Adult whipworms live in the large intestine and feed off of a dog's blood. Whipworm infections are not as easy to detect as with other types of internal parasites, since eggs are not constantly shed by the dog. Symptoms include diarrhea that often contains fresh blood, vomiting and weight loss. Whipworms, like roundworms, are transmitted when a dog ingests eggs that are shed in feces. These eggs can also live in soil, where a dog can pick up the parasite, for years.

HOOKWORMS

Hookworms live in the small intestine of their hosts and ingest blood for nourishment. Hookworm infestation is often first detected by bloody diarrhea and a general failure to thrive. Hookworms are transmitted through the stool of infected animals and can either be ingested or can attach themselves to the feet of their new hosts and burrow their way into the skin. Hookworms can also infect humans who come in contact with infested soil by walking barefoot.

HEARTWORM

Heartworm is one of the most serious and life-threatening of all canine internal parasites. Adult heartworms live in the heart and larger pulmonary arteries where they weaken circulation as they damage valuable tissue. Poor circulation results, which in turn causes damage to other bodily functions.

The intermediate host for heartworms is the mosquito, which sucks up the microfilaria (larvae) of the heartworm from one animal and transmits it to the next dog that it bites. Dogs infected with heartworm can be successfully treated if the infestation is caught in its early stages. The chemical treatment for this parasite is highly toxic and can itself be fatal. Careful treatment includes weeks of crate rest while the animal recovers from infestation. Preventative medication is available in either a daily or a monthly form and should be administered per recommendation of your veterinarian.

The use of Ivermectin-based preventatives is contraindicated in Collie breeds because of their sensitivity to the drug. However, despite their Collie ancestry, the Australian Cattle Dog does not appear to have a negative reaction to Ivermectin.

INTESTINAL PROTOZOA

Coccidia and Giardia are intestinal protozoa that cause persistent intermittent diarrhea in canines. Giardia are common to wild animals in many areas, so your Australian Cattle Dog can pick it up from drinking from a water source where wild animals are living. Detection of this type of infestation can be difficult and must be done by microscopic investigation of a fresh fecal sample. Veterinary treatment is necessary to counteract the effects of dehydration and to eradicate the protozoa.

Medical Conditions That Commonly Affect Australian Cattle Dogs

HIP DYSPLASIA

Simply put, hip dysplasia (HD) is a developmental disorder that occurs when the head of the femur (thigh bone) and the acetabulum (hip socket) do not fit together properly. Genetics play a large part in the development of HD, but recent studies show that environment, exercise and diet may also play a role. This disorder can be exceptionally debilitating, and corrective surgery can cost thousands of dollars. Care should be taken to purchase puppies only from stock that has been x-rayed and given a passing rating (either "excellent," "good" or "fair") by the Orthopedic Foundation for Animals (OFA).

PROGRESSIVE RETINAL ATROPHY

Progressive retinal atrophy (PRA) is a degenerative disease of the eye that eventually leads to blindness. While PRA in Australian Cattle Dogs was thought to occur later in life (at six to seven years of age), dogs as young as six months old have recently been found with this disorder. The first sign that a dog may be affected by PRA is the loss of acute vision in the early evening or at dusk. Breeding animals should be tested by a veterinary ophthalmologist and cleared annually by the Canine Eye Research Foundation (CERF). Affected animals should be taken out of a breeding program and known carriers should be used with extreme caution. A blood test that will actually pinpoint carriers of this potentially devastating disorder is currently being developed. Hopefully, in the next ten years or so great strides will be made in eradicating progressive retinal atrophy in the Australian Cattle Dog.

DEAFNESS

While little is known about the inheritance of deafness in the Australian Cattle Dog, the anomaly is presumed to have come from the infusion of Dalmatian and/or Bull Terrier into the breed. It is often difficult to detect a deaf pup while it is still with its littermates, but a Brainstem Auditory Evoked Response test (BAER) can be performed on any dog suspected of being deaf. Puppies that are unilaterally deaf can lead near-normal lives with only minor difficulties in sound localization. Bilaterally deaf puppies are very difficult to place into a home that cares enough to attend to their special training needs, and are generally humanely euthanized.

Spaying and Neutering

Thousands of unwanted animals are euthanized yearly. There is a never-ending list of Australian Cattle Dogs in regional or national rescue programs that are looking for homes, and who are sometimes euthanized when one is not available. Statistics show that the risk of testicular, ovarian and mammary tumors is greatly diminished if your dog is altered at an early age.

THE NEUTERED MALE

Neutering your Australian Cattle Dog will make your life easier and your dog's life healthier. A male dog who is neutered (castrated) at a young age will be less apt to develop aggressive tendencies and to roam. A neutered male will also be much less likely to urinate in order to mark his territory.

THE SPAYED FEMALE

A female in season can not only create an awful mess in the house, but will also attract males from all over the neighborhood. A spayed female will, of course, not go through these heat cycles.

Breeding

If no one was interested in reproducing generations of dogs with similar characteristics, purebred dogs would not exist. Breeding is a great responsibility, however, and should not be taken lightly. While many people have a simplistic view of "the miracle of life," the truth is that so many things can go wrong in planning, breeding and whelping a litter that the process is best left to those who have studied the breed and its genetics for years before actually breeding.

BIG BUCKS

A responsibly planned litter can cost several thousand dollars to breed. Both sire and dam of a prospective litter should be proven to conform to the breed standard by earning their Championships. They should also earn working titles to show that their instinct and bidability are true to the heritage of the breed. The sire and dam of the litter should also have their hips tested and graded by OFA, their eyes checked annually and certified by CERF, and their hearing tested.

ADVANTAGES OF SPAY/NEUTER

The greatest advantage of spaying (for females) or neutering (for males) your dog is that you are guaranteed your dog will not produce puppies. There are too many puppies already available for too few homes. There are other advantages as well.

ADVANTAGES OF SPAYING

No messy heats.

No "suitors" howling at your windows or waiting in your yard.

Decreased incidences of pyometra (disease of the uterus) and breast cancer.

ADVANTAGES OF NEUTERING

Lessens male aggressive and territorial behaviors, but doesn't affect the dog's personality. Behaviors are often owner-induced, so neutering is not the only answer, but it is a good start.

Prevents the need to roam in search of bitches in season.

Decreased incidences of urogenital diseases.

A Lifetime of Commitment

Remember that bringing puppies into this world should mean that you are willing to take responsibility for an entire lifetime. Despite all of the genetic tests and research, problems can crop up even in well-planned litters. I have told people dozens of times that if one of the dogs in my home were to go blind or become crippled tomorrow, I would be extremely sad. If one of the people who have adopted one of my puppies had a similar problem with his or her dog, I would be devastated. The responsibility of bringing puppies into this world is an awesome one. Breeding without thinking about certain factors is not only irresponsible, it is also a great disservice to the breed. Those who truly love and care about the Australian Cattle Dog want to preserve its characteristics and want to eradicate the genetic disorders that are seen in the breed today.

Pups are really cute—but think twice before breeding your Australian Cattle Dog.

The Aging Australian Cattle Dog

The Australian Cattle Dog generally lives a long and healthy life. Many Australian Cattle Dogs begin to show the first signs of slowing by age ten or so. The aging

Australian Cattle Dog may become a bit arthritic and
his vision may become cloudy due to senile cataracts,
but his joy for life and creative thinking never seem to
diminish.

WEIGHT GAIN

You should watch the weight of your Australian Cattle
Dog carefully as he ages and consequently burns fewer
calories. Your dog will need to consume fewer calories
and less protein as his activity level slows down and his
body ages. Extra weight constitutes added stress on the
already creaking joints.

SAYING GOOD-BYE

Elderly Australian Cattle Dogs rarely linger before
death. Most simply go to sleep in their favorite places
and do not wake up in the morning.

EUTHANASIA

One of the most difficult decisions a dog owner will
ever make is when to humanely relieve his or her
dog of his pain and suffering. Keep in mind that
euthanasia is merely an overdose of anesthetic that
causes your beloved companion to drift off to deep
sleep before he quietly stops breathing. When that
time comes, have the strength to be with your dog.
Hold him, hug him and talk to him quietly so that
the last voice he hears on this earth is the voice of
his loving owner. At the time, it may seem the most
difficult thing to do, but you will eventually look back
on the experience and know that your beloved companion left this world in the arms of someone who
truly loved him.

TAKE TIME TO HEAL

A well-loved dog is an emotional investment of unpar-
alleled returns. Unfortunately, our dogs' lives are too
short, and we inevitably must cope with losing them.
Grief is a natural reaction to the loss of a pet.

Give yourself time to grieve the loss of your companion. If you think it will help, have a ceremony to bury your Australian Cattle Dog or spread his or her ashes in a favorite spot.

Your Happy, Healthy Pet

Your Dog's Name _____

Name on Your Dog's Pedigree (if your dog has one) _____

_____

Where Your Dog Came From _____

_____

Your Dog's Birthday _____

Your Dog's Veterinarian

    Name _____

    Address _____

    Phone Number_____

    Emergency Number_____

Your Dog's Health

    Vaccines

    type _____ date given _____

    type _____ date given _____

    type _____ date given _____

    type _____ date given _____

    Heartworm

    date tested _____ type used_____ start date _____

Your Dog's License Number_____

Groomer's Name and Number _____

Dogsitter/Walker's Name and Number_____

Awards Your Dog Has Won

    Award _____ date earned _____

    Award _____ date earned _____

part three

Enjoying
your
Dog

chapter 8

Basic
Training

by Ian Dunbar, Ph.D., MRCVS

Training is the jewel in the crown—the most important aspect of doggy husbandry. There is no more important variable influencing dog behavior and temperament than the dog's education: A well-trained, well-behaved and good-natured puppydog is always a joy to live with, but an untrained and uncivilized dog can be a perpetual nightmare. Moreover, deny the dog an education and it will not have the opportunity to fulfill its own canine potential; neither will it have the ability to communicate effectively with its human companions.

Luckily, modern psychological training methods are easy, efficient and effective and, above all, considerably dog-friendly and user-friendly. Doggy education is as simple as it is enjoyable. But before you can have a good time play-training with your new dog, you have to learn what to do and how to do it. There is no bigger variable influencing the success of dog training than the *owner's* experience and expertise. *Before you embark on the dog's education, you must first educate yourself.*

Basic Training for Owners

Ideally, basic owner training should begin well *before* you select your dog. Find out all you can about your chosen breed first, then master rudimentary training and handling skills. If you already have your puppy/dog, owner training is a dire emergency—the clock is running! Especially for puppies, the first few weeks at home are the most important and influential days in the dog's life. Indeed, the cause of most adolescent and adult problems may be traced back to the initial days the pup explores his new home. This is the time to establish the *status quo*—to teach the puppy/dog how you would like him to behave and so prevent otherwise quite predictable problems.

In addition to consulting breeders and breed books such as this one (which understandably have a positive breed bias), seek out as many pet owners with your breed you can find. Good points are obvious. What you want to find out are the breed-specific *problems*, so you can nip them in the bud. In particular, you should talk to owners with *adolescent* dogs and make a list of all anticipated problems. Most important, *test drive* at least half a dozen adolescent and adult dogs of your breed yourself. An eight-week-old puppy is deceptively easy to handle, but she will acquire adult size, speed and strength in just four months, so you should learn now what to prepare for.

Puppy and pet dog training classes offer a convenient venue to locate pet owners and observe dogs in action. For a list of suitable trainers in your area, contact the Association of Pet Dog Trainers (see Chapter 13). You may also begin your basic owner training by observing other owners in class. Watch as many classes and test drive as many dogs as possible. Select an upbeat, dog-friendly, people-friendly, fun-and-games, puppydog pet training class to learn the ropes. Also, watch training videos and read training books (see Chapter 12). You must find out what to do and how to do it *before* you have to do it.

Principles of Training

Most people think training comprises teaching the dog to do things such as sit, speak and roll over, but even a four-week-old pup knows how to do these things already. Instead, the first step in training involves teaching the dog human words for each dog behavior and activity and for each aspect of the dog's environment. That way you, the owner, can more easily participate in the dog's domestic education by directing him to perform specific actions appropriately, that is, at the right time, in the right place, and so on. Training opens communication channels, enabling an educated dog to at least understand the owner's requests.

In addition to teaching a dog *what* we want her to do, it is also necessary to teach her *why* she should do what we ask. Indeed, 95 percent of training revolves around motivating the dog *to want to do* what we want. Dogs often understand what their owners want; they just don't see the point of doing it—especially when the owner's repetitively boring and seemingly senseless instructions are totally at odds with much more pressing and exciting doggy distractions. It is not so much the dog who is being stubborn or dominant; rather, it is the owner who has failed to acknowledge the dog's needs and feelings and to approach training from the dog's point of view.

The Meaning of Instructions

The secret to successful training is learning how to use training lures to predict or prompt specific behaviors—to coax the dog to do what you want *when* you want. Any highly valued object (such as a treat or toy) may be used as a lure, which the dog will follow with his eyes and nose. Moving the lure in specific ways entices the dog to move his nose, head and entire body in specific ways. In fact, by learning the art of manipulating various lures, it is possible to teach the dog to assume virtually any body position and perform any action. Once you have control over the expression of the dog's behaviors and can elicit any body position or behavior at will, you can easily teach the dog to perform on request.

Tell your dog what you want him to do, use a lure to entice him to respond correctly, then profusely praise

Teach your dog words for each activity he needs to know, like down.

and maybe reward him once he performs the desired action. For example, verbally request "Fido, sit!" while you move a squeaky toy upwards and backwards over the dog's muzzle (lure-movement and hand signal), smile knowingly as he looks up (to follow the lure) and sits down (as a result of canine anatomical engineering), then praise him to distraction ("Gooood Fido!"). Squeak the toy, offer a training treat and give your dog and yourself a pat on the back.

Being able to elicit desired responses over and over enables the owner to reward the dog over and over. Consequently, the dog begins to think training is fun. For example, the more the dog is rewarded for sitting, the more she enjoys sitting. Eventually the dog comes to realize that, whereas most sitting is appreciated, sitting immediately upon request usually prompts especially enthusiastic praise and a slew of high-level rewards. The dog begins to sit on cue much of the time, showing that she is starting to grasp the meaning of the owner's verbal request and hand signal.

Why Comply?

Most dogs enjoy initial lure/reward training and are only too happy to comply with their owners' wishes. Unfortunately, repetitive drilling without appreciative feedback tends to diminish the dog's enthusiasm until he eventually fails to see the point of complying anymore. Moreover, as the dog approaches adolescence he becomes more easily distracted as he develops other interests. Lengthy sessions with repetitive exercises tend to bore and demotivate both parties. If it's not fun, the owner doesn't do it and neither does the dog.

Integrate training into your dog's life: The greater number of training sessions each day and the *shorter* they are, the more willingly compliant your dog will become. Make sure to have a short (just a few seconds) training interlude before every enjoyable canine activity. For example, ask your dog to sit to greet people, to sit before you throw his Frisbee, and to sit for his supper. Really, sitting is no different from a canine "please." Also, include numerous short training interludes during every enjoyable canine pastime, for example, when playing with the dog or when he is running in the park. In this fashion, doggy distractions may be effectively converted into rewards for training. Just as all games have rules, fun becomes training . . . and training becomes fun.

Eventually, rewards actually become unnecessary to continue motivating your dog. If trained with consideration and kindness, performing the desired behaviors will become self-rewarding and, in a sense, your dog will motivate himself. Just as it is not necessary to reward a human companion during an enjoyable walk in the park, or following a game of tennis, it is hardly necessary to reward our best friend—the dog—for walking by our side or while playing fetch. Human company during enjoyable activities is reward enough for most dogs.

Even though your dog has become self-motivating, it's still good to praise and pet him a lot and offer rewards once in a while, especially for a good job well done. And if for no other reason, praising and rewarding others is good for the human heart.

To train your dog, you need gentle hands, a loving heart and a good attitude.

Punishment

Without a doubt, lure/reward training is by far the best way to teach: Entice your dog to do what you want and then reward him for doing so. Unfortunately, a human shortcoming is to take the good for granted and to moan and groan at the bad. Specifically, the dog's many good behaviors are ignored while the owner focuses on punishing the dog for making mistakes. In extreme cases, instruction is *limited* to punishing mistakes made by a trainee dog, child, employee or husband, even though it has been proven punishment training is notoriously inefficient and ineffective and is decidedly unfriendly and combative. It teaches the dog that training is a drag, almost as quickly as it teaches the dog to dislike his trainer. Why treat our best friends like our worst enemies?

Punishment training is also much more laborious and time consuming. Whereas it takes only a finite amount of time to teach a dog what to chew, for example, it takes much, much longer to punish the dog for each and every mistake. Remember, *there is only one right way!* So why not teach that right way from the outset?!

To make matters worse, punishment training causes severe lapses in the dog's reliability. Since it is obviously impossible to punish the dog each and every time she misbehaves, the dog quickly learns to distinguish between those times when she must comply (so as to avoid impending punishment) and those times when she need not comply, because punishment is impossible. Such times include when the dog is off leash and only six feet away, when the owner is otherwise engaged (talking to a friend, watching television, taking a shower, tending to the baby or chatting on the telephone), or when the dog is left at home alone.

Instances of misbehavior will be numerous when the owner is away, because even when the dog complied in the owner's looming presence, he did so unwillingly. The dog was forced to act against his will, rather than moulding his will to want to please. Hence, when the owner is absent, not only does the dog know he need not comply, he simply does not want to. Again, the trainee is not a stubborn vindictive beast, but rather the trainer has failed to teach.

Punishment training invariably creates unpredictable Jekyll and Hyde behavior.

Trainer's Tools

Many training books extol the virtues of a vast array of training paraphernalia and electronic and metallic gizmos, most of which are designed for canine restraint, correction and punishment, rather than for actual facilitation of doggy education. In reality, most effective training tools are not found in stores; they come from within ourselves. In addition to a willing dog, all you really need is a functional human brain, gentle hands, a loving heart and a good attitude.

In terms of equipment, all dogs do require a quality buckle collar to sport dog tags and to attach the leash (for safety and to comply with local leash laws). Hollow chewtoys (like Kongs or sterilized longbones) and a dog bed or collapsible crate are a must for housetraining. Three additional tools are required:

1. specific lures (training treats and toys) to predict and prompt specific desired behaviors;

2. rewards (praise, affection, training treats and toys) to reinforce for the dog what a lot of fun it all is; and

3. knowledge—how to convert the dog's favorite activities and games (potential distractions to training) into "life-rewards," which may be employed to facilitate training.

The most powerful of these is *knowledge*. Education is the key! Watch training classes, participate in training classes, watch videos, read books, enjoy playtraining with your dog, and then your dog will say "Please," and your dog will say "Thank you!"

Housetraining

If dogs were left to their own devices, certainly they would chew, dig and bark for entertainment and then no doubt highlight a few areas of their living space with sprinkles of urine, in much the same way we decorate by hanging pictures. Consequently, when we ask a dog to live with us, we must teach him *where* he may dig and perform his toilet duties, *what* he may chew and *when* he may bark. After all, when left at home alone for many hours, we cannot expect the dog to amuse himself by completing crosswords or watching the soaps on TV!

Also, it would be decidedly unfair to keep the house rules a secret from the dog, and then get angry and punish the poor critter for inevitably transgressing rules he did not even know existed. Remember, without adequate education and guidance, the dog will be forced to establish his own rules—doggy rules—that most probably will be at odds with the owner's view of domestic living.

Since most problems develop during the first few days the dog is at home, prospective dog owners must be certain they are quite clear about the principles of housetraining *before* they get a dog. Early misbehaviors quickly become established as the status quo—

becoming firmly entrenched as hard-to-break bad habits, which set the precedent for years to come. Make sure to teach your dog good habits right from the start. Good habits are just as hard to break as bad ones!

Ideally, when a new dog comes home, try to arrange for someone to be present for as much as possible during the first few days (for adult dogs) or weeks for puppies. With only a little forethought, it is surprisingly easy to find a puppy sitter, such as a retired person, who would be willing to eat from your refrigerator and watch your television while keeping an eye on the newcomer to encourage the dog to play with chewtoys and to ensure he goes outside on a regular basis.

POTTY TRAINING

To teach the dog where to relieve himself:

1. never let him make a single mistake;

2. let him know where you want him to go; and

3. handsomely reward him for doing so: "GOOOOOOOD DOG!!!" liver treat, liver treat, liver treat!

PREVENTING MISTAKES

A single mistake is a training disaster, since it heralds many more in future weeks. And each time the dog soils the house, this further reinforces the dog's unfortunate preference for an indoor, carpeted toilet. *Do not let an unhousetrained dog have full run of the house if you are away from home or cannot pay full attention.* Instead, confine the dog to an area where elimination is appropriate, such as an outdoor run or, better still, a small, comfortable indoor kennel with access to an outdoor run. When confined in this manner, most dogs will naturally housetrain themselves.

If that's not possible, confine the dog to an area, such as a utility room, kitchen, basement or garage, where elimination may not be desired in the long run but as an interim measure it is certainly preferable to doing it all around the house. Use newspaper to cover the floor of the dog's day room. The newspaper may be used to soak up the urine and to wrap up and dispose of the feces. Once your dog develops a preferred spot for eliminating, it is only necessary to cover that part of the floor with newspaper. The smaller papered area may then be moved (only a little each day) towards the door to the outside. Thus the dog will develop the tendency to go to the door when he needs to relieve himself.

The first few weeks at home are the most important and influential in your dog's life.

Never confine an unhousetrained dog to a crate for long periods. Doing so would force the dog to soil the crate and ruin its usefulness as an aid for housetraining (see the following discussion).

Teaching Where

In order to teach your dog where you would like her to do her business, you have to be there to direct the proceedings—an obvious, yet often neglected, fact of life. In order to be there to teach the dog *where* to go, you need to know *when* she needs to go. Indeed, the success of housetraining depends on the owner's ability to predict these times. Certainly, a regular feeding schedule will facilitate prediction somewhat, but there is nothing like "loading the deck" and influencing the timing of the outcome yourself!

Whenever you are at home, make sure the dog is under constant supervision and/or confined to a small area. If already well trained, simply instruct the dog to lie down in his bed or basket. Alternatively, confine the dog to a crate (doggy den) or tie-down (a short, 18-inch lead that can be clipped to an eye hook in the baseboard). Short-term close confinement strongly inhibits urination and defecation, since the dog does not want to soil his sleeping area. Thus, when you release the puppydog each hour, he will definitely need to urinate immediately and defecate every third or fourth hour. Keep the dog confined to his doggy den and take him to his intended toilet area each hour, every hour, and on the hour.

When taking your dog outside, instruct him to sit quietly before opening the door—he will soon learn to sit by the door when he needs to go out!

TEACHING WHY

Being able to predict when the dog needs to go enables the owner to be on the spot to praise and reward the dog. Each hour, hurry the dog to the intended toilet area in the yard, issue the appropriate instruction ("Go pee!" or "Go poop!"), then give the dog three to four minutes to produce. Praise and offer a couple of training treats when successful. The treats are important because many people fail to praise their dogs with feeling . . . and housetraining is hardly the time for understatement. So either loosen up and enthusiastically praise that dog: "Wuzzzer-wuzzer-wuzzer, hoooser good wuffer den? Hoooo went pee for Daddy?" Or say "Good dog!" as best you can and offer the treats for effect.

Following elimination is an ideal time for a spot of playtraining in the yard or house. Also, an empty dog may be allowed greater freedom around the house for the next half hour or so, just as long as you keep an eye out to make sure he does not get into other kinds of mischief. If you are preoccupied and cannot pay full attention, confine the dog to his doggy den once more to enjoy a peaceful snooze or to play with his many chewtoys.

If your dog does not eliminate within the allotted time outside—no biggie! Back to his doggy den, and then try again after another hour.

As I own large dogs, I always feel more relaxed walking an empty dog, knowing that I will not need to finish our stroll weighted down with bags of feces! Beware of falling into the trap of walking the dog to get it to eliminate. The good ol' dog walk is such an enormous highlight in the dog's life that it represents the single biggest potential reward in domestic dogdom. However, when in a hurry, or during inclement weather, many owners abruptly terminate the walk the moment the dog has done its business. This, in effect, severely punishes the dog for doing the right thing, in the right place at the right time. Consequently, many dogs become strongly inhibited from eliminating outdoors because they know it will signal an abrupt end to an otherwise thoroughly enjoyable walk.

Instead, instruct the dog to relieve himself in the yard prior to going for a walk. If you follow the above instructions, most dogs soon learn to eliminate on cue. As soon as the dog eliminates, praise (and offer a treat or two)—"Good dog! Let's go walkies!" Use the walk as a reward for eliminating in the yard. If the dog does not go, put him back in his doggy den and think about a walk later on. You will find with a "No feces–no walk" policy, your dog will become one of the fastest defecators in the business.

If you do not have a back yard, instruct the dog to eliminate right outside your front door prior to the walk. Not only will this facilitate clean up and disposal of the feces in your own trash can but, also, the walk may again be used as a colossal reward.

CHEWING AND BARKING

Short-term close confinement also teaches the dog that occasional quiet moments are a reality of domestic living. Your puppydog is extremely impressionable during his first few weeks at home. Regular confinement at this time soon exerts a calming influence over the dog's personality. Remember, once the dog is housetrained and calmer, there will be a whole lifetime ahead for the dog to enjoy full run of the house and garden. On the other hand, by letting the newcomer have unrestricted access to the entire household and allowing him to run willy-nilly, he will most certainly develop a bunch of behavior problems in short order, no doubt necessitating confinement later in life. It would not be fair to remedially restrain and confine a dog you have trained, through neglect, to run free.

When confining the dog, make sure he always has an impressive array of suitable chewtoys. Kongs and sterilized longbones (both readily available from pet stores) make the best chewtoys, since they are hollow and may be stuffed with treats to heighten the dog's interest. For example, by stuffing the little hole at the top of a Kong with a small piece of freeze-dried liver, the dog will not want to leave it alone.

Remember, treats do not have to be junk food and they certainly should not represent extra calories. Rather, treats should be part of each dog's regular daily diet:

Make sure your puppy has suitable chewtoys.

Some food may be served in the dog's bowl for breakfast and dinner, some food may be used as training treats, and some food may be used for stuffing chewtoys. I regularly stuff my dogs' many Kongs with different shaped biscuits and kibble. The kibble seems to fall out fairly easily, as do the oval-shaped biscuits, thus rewarding the dog instantaneously for checking out the chewtoys. The bone-shaped biscuits fall out after a while, rewarding the dog for worrying at the chewtoy. But the triangular biscuits never come out. They remain inside the Kong as lures, maintaining the dog's fascination with its chewtoy. To further focus the dog's interest, I always make sure to flavor the triangular biscuits by rubbing them with a little cheese or freeze-dried liver.

If stuffed chewtoys are reserved especially for times the dog is confined, the puppydog will soon learn to enjoy quiet moments in her doggy den and she will quickly develop a chewtoy habit—a good habit! This is a simple *passive training* process; all the owner has to do is set up the situation and the dog all but trains herself—easy and effective. Even when the dog is given run of the house, her first inclination will be to indulge her rewarding chewtoy habit rather than destroying less-attractive household articles, such as curtains, carpets, chairs and compact disks. Similarly, a chewtoy chewer will be less inclined to scratch and chew herself excessively. Also, if the dog busies herself as a recreational chewer, she will be less inclined to develop into a recreational barker or digger when left at home alone.

Stuff a number of chewtoys whenever the dog is left confined and remove the extra-special-tasting treats when you return. Your dog will now amuse himself with his chewtoys before falling asleep and then resume playing with his chewtoys when he expects you to return. Since most owner-absent misbehavior happens right after you leave and right before your expected return, your puppydog will now be conveniently preoccupied with his chewtoys at these times.

To teach come, call your dog, open your arms as a welcoming signal, wave a toy or a treat and praise for every step in your direction.

Come and Sit

Most puppies will happily approach virtually anyone, whether called or not; that is, until they collide with adolescence and develop other more important doggy interests, such as sniffing a multiplicity of exquisite odors on the grass. Your mission, Mr. and/or Ms. Owner, is to teach and reward the pup for coming reliably, willingly and happily when called—and you have just three months to get it done. Unless adequately reinforced, your puppy's tendency to approach people will self-destruct by adolescence.

Call your dog ("Fido, come!"), open your arms (and maybe squat down) as a welcoming signal, waggle a treat or toy as a lure, and reward the puppydog when he comes running. Do not wait to praise the dog until he reaches you—he may come 95 percent of the way and then run off after some distraction. Instead, praise the dog's *first* step towards you and continue praising enthusiastically for *every* step he takes in your direction.

When the rapidly approaching puppy dog is three lengths away from impact, instruct him to sit ("Fido, sit!") and hold the lure in front of you in an outstretched hand to prevent him from hitting you midchest and knocking you flat on your back! As Fido decelerates to nose the lure, move the treat upwards and backwards just over his muzzle with an upwards motion of your extended arm (palm-upwards). As the dog looks up to follow the lure, he will sit down (if he jumps up, you are holding the lure too high). Praise the dog for sitting. Move backwards and call him again. Repeat this many times over, always praising when Fido comes and sits; on occasion, reward him.

For the first couple of trials, use a training treat both as a lure to entice the dog to come and sit and as a reward for doing so. Thereafter, try to use different items as lures and rewards. For example, lure the dog with a Kong or Frisbee but reward her with a food treat. Or lure the dog with a food treat but pat her and throw a tennis ball as a reward. After just a few repetitions, dispense with the lures and rewards; the dog will begin to respond willingly to your verbal requests and hand signals just for the prospect of praise from your heart and affection from your hands.

Instruct every family member, friend and visitor how to get the dog to come and sit. Invite people over for a series of pooch parties; do not keep the pup a secret—let other people enjoy this puppy, and let the pup enjoy other people. Puppydog parties are not only fun, they easily attract a lot of people to help *you* train *your* dog. Unless you teach your dog *how* to meet people, that is, to sit for greetings, no doubt the dog will resort to jumping up. Then you and the visitors will get annoyed, and the dog will be punished. This is not fair. *Send out those invitations for puppy parties and teach your dog to be mannerly and socially acceptable.*

Even though your dog quickly masters obedient recalls in the house, his reliability may falter when playing in the back yard or local park. Ironically, it is *the owner* who has unintentionally trained the dog *not* to respond in these instances. By allowing the dog to play and run around and otherwise have a good time, but then to call the dog to put him on leash to take him home, the dog quickly learns playing is fun but training is a drag. Thus, playing in the park becomes a severe distraction, which works against training. Bad news!

Instead, whether playing with the dog off leash or on leash, request him to come at frequent intervals—say, every minute or so. On most occasions, praise and pet the dog for a few seconds while he is sitting, then tell him to go play again. For especially fast recalls, offer a couple of training treats and take the time to praise and pet the dog enthusiastically before releasing him. The dog will learn that coming when called is not necessarily the end of the play session, and neither is it the end of the world; rather, it signals an enjoyable, quality time-out with the owner before resuming play once more. In fact, playing in the park now becomes a very effective life-reward, which works to facilitate training by reinforcing each obedient and timely recall. Good news!

Sit, Down, Stand and Rollover

Teaching the dog a variety of body positions is easy for owner and dog, impressive for spectators and extremely useful for all. Using lure-reward techniques, it is possible to train several positions at once to verbal commands or hand signals (which impress the socks off onlookers).

Sit and *down*—the two control commands—prevent or resolve nearly a hundred behavior problems. For example, if the dog happily and obediently sits or lies down when requested, he cannot jump on visitors, dash out the front door, run around and chase its tail, pester other dogs, harass cats or annoy family, friends or strangers. Additionally, "sit" or "down" are better emergency commands for off-leash control.

It is easier to teach and maintain a reliable sit than maintain a reliable recall. *Sit* is the purest and simplest of commands—either the dog is sitting or he is not. If there is any change of circumstances or potential danger in the park, for example, simply instruct the dog to sit. If he sits, you have a number of options: allow the dog to resume playing when he is safe; walk up and put the dog on leash, or call the dog. The dog will be much more likely to come when called if he has already acknowledged his compliance by sitting. If the dog does not sit in the park—train him to!

Stand and *rollover-stay* are the two positions for examining the dog. Your veterinarian will love you to distraction if you take a little time to teach the dog to stand still and roll over and play possum. Also, your vet bills will be smaller. The rollover-stay is an especially useful command and is really just a variation of the down-stay: whereas the dog lies prone in the traditional down, she lies supine in the rollover-stay.

As with teaching come and sit, the training techniques to teach the dog to assume all other body positions on cue are user-friendly and dog-friendly. Simply give the appropriate request, lure the dog into the desired body position using a training treat or toy and then *praise* (and maybe reward) the dog as soon as he complies. Try not to touch the dog to get him to respond. If you teach the dog by guiding him into position, the dog will quickly learn that rump-pressure means sit, for example, but as yet you still have no control over your dog if he is just six feet away. It will still be necessary to teach the dog to sit on request. So do not make training a time-consuming two-step process; instead, teach the dog to sit to a verbal request or hand signal from the outset. Once the dog sits willingly when requested, by all means use your hands to pet the dog when he does so.

To teach *down* when the dog is already sitting, say "Fido, down!," hold the lure in one hand (palm down) and lower that hand to the floor between the dog's forepaws. As the dog lowers his head to follow the lure, slowly move the lure away from the dog just a fraction (in front of his paws). The dog will lie down as he stretches his nose forward to follow the lure. Praise the dog when he does so. If the dog stands up, you pulled the lure away too far and too quickly.

When teaching the dog to lie down from the standing position, say "down" and lower the lure to the floor as before. Once the dog has lowered his forequarters and assumed a play bow, gently and slowly move the lure *towards* the dog between his forelegs. Praise the dog as soon as his rear end plops down.

After just a couple of trials it will be possible to alternate sits and downs and have the dog energetically perform doggy push-ups. Praise the dog a lot, and after half a dozen or so push-ups reward the dog with a training treat or toy. You will notice the more energetically you move your arm—upwards (palm up) to get the dog to sit, and downwards (palm down) to get the dog to lie down—the more energetically the dog responds to your requests. Now try training the dog in silence and you will notice he has also learned to respond to hand signals. Yeah! Not too shabby for the first session.

To teach *stand* from the sitting position, say "Fido, stand," slowly move the lure half a dog-length away from the dog's nose, keeping it at nose level, and praise the dog as he stands to follow the lure. As soon

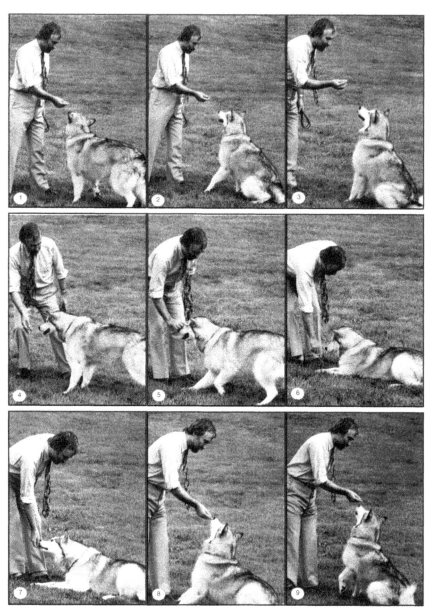

Using a food lure to teach sit, down and stand. 1) "Phoenix, Sit." 2) Hand palm upwards, move lure up and back over dog's muzzle. 3) "Good sit, Phoenix!" 4) "Phoenix, down." 5) Hand palm downwards, move lure down to lie between dog's forepaws. 6) "Phoenix, off. Good down, Phoenix!" 7) "Phoenix, sit!" 8) Palm upwards, move lure up and back, keeping it close to dog's muzzle. 9) "Good sit, Phoenix!"

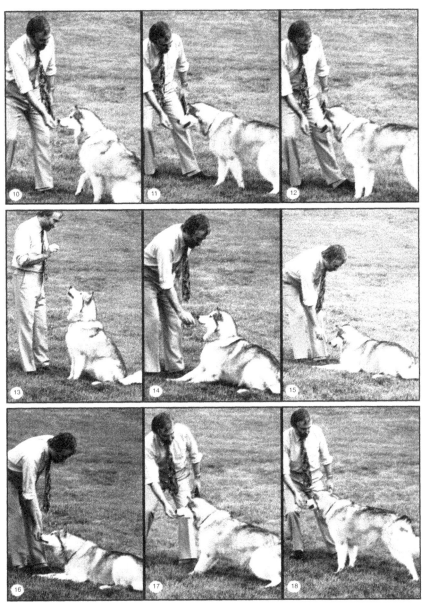

10) "Phoenix, stand!" 11) Move lure away from dog at nose height, then lower it a tad. 12) "Phoenix, off! Good stand, Phoenix!" 13) "Phoenix, down!" 14) Hand palm downwards, move lure down to lie between dog's forepaws. 15) "Phoenix, off! Good down-stay, Phoenix!" 16) "Phoenix, stand!" 17) Move lure away from dog's muzzle up to nose height. 18) "Phoenix, off! Good stand-stay, Phoenix. Now we'll make the vet and groomer happy!"

as the dog stands, lower the lure to just beneath the dog's chin to entice him to look down; otherwise he will stand and then sit immediately. To prompt the dog to stand from the down position, move the lure half a dog-length upwards and away from the dog, holding the lure at standing nose height from the floor.

Teaching *rollover* is best started from the down position, with the dog lying on one side, or at least with both hind legs stretched out on the same side. Say "Fido, bang!" and move the lure backwards and alongside the dog's muzzle to its elbow (on the side of its outstretched hind legs). Once the dog looks to the side and backwards, very slowly move the lure upwards to the dog's shoulder and backbone. Tickling the dog in the goolies (groin area) often invokes a reflex-raising of the hind leg as an appeasement gesture, which facilitates the tendency to roll over. If you move the lure too quickly and the dog jumps into the standing position, have patience and start again. As soon as the dog rolls onto its back, keep the lure stationary and mesmerize the dog with a relaxing tummy rub.

To teach *rollover-stay* when the dog is standing or moving, say "Fido, bang!" and give the appropriate hand signal (with index finger pointed and thumb cocked in true Sam Spade fashion), then in one fluid movement lure him to first lie down and then rollover-stay as above.

Teaching the dog to *stay* in each of the above four positions becomes a piece of cake after first teaching the dog not to worry at the toy or treat training lure. This is best accomplished by hand feeding dinner kibble. Hold a piece of kibble firmly in your hand and softly instruct "Off!" Ignore any licking and slobbering *for however long the dog worries at the treat*, but say "Take it!" and offer the kibble *the instant* the dog breaks contact with his muzzle. Repeat this a few times, and then up the ante and insist the dog remove his muzzle for one whole second before offering the kibble. Then progressively refine your criteria and have the dog not touch your hand (or treat) for longer and longer periods on each trial, such as for two seconds, four seconds, then six, ten, fifteen, twenty, thirty seconds and so on. The dog soon learns: (1) worrying at the treat never gets results, whereas (2) noncontact is often rewarded after a variable time lapse.

Teaching *"Off!"* has many useful applications in its own right. Additionally, instructing the dog not to touch a training lure often produces spontaneous and magical stays. Request the dog to stand-stay, for example, and not to touch the lure. At first set your sights on a short two-second stay before rewarding the dog. (Remember, every long journey begins with a single step.) However, on subsequent trials, gradually and progressively increase the length of stay required to receive a reward. In no time at all your dog will stand calmly for a minute or so.

Relevancy Training

Once you have taught the dog what you expect her to do when requested to come, sit, lie down, stand, rollover and stay, the time is right to teach the dog *why* she should comply with your wishes. The secret is to have many (*many*) extremely short training interludes (two to five seconds each) at numerous (*numerous*) times during the course of the dog's day. Especially work with the dog immediately *before* the dog's good times and *during* the dog's good times. For example, ask your dog to sit and/or lie down each time before opening doors, serving meals, offering treats, tummy rubs; ask the dog to perform a few controlled doggy push-ups before letting her off-leash or throwing a tennis ball; and perhaps request the dog to sit-down-sit-stand-down-stand-rollover before inviting her to cuddle on the couch.

Similarly, request the dog to sit many times during play or on walks, and in no time at all the dog will be only too pleased to follow your instructions because he has learned that a compliant response heralds all sorts of goodies. Basically all you are trying to teach the dog is how to say please: "Please throw the tennis ball. Please may I snuggle on the couch."

Remember, whereas it is important to keep training interludes short, it is equally important to have many short sessions each and every day. The shortest (and most useful) session comprises asking the dog to sit and then go play during a play session. When trained this way, your dog will soon associate training with good times. In fact, the dog may be unable to distinguish between training and good times and, indeed, there should be no distinction. The warped concept that training involves forcing the dog to comply and/or dominating his will is totally at odds with the picture of a truly well-trained dog. In reality, enjoying a game of training with a dog is no different from enjoying a game of backgammon or tennis with a friend; and walking with a dog should be no different from strolling with buddies on the golf course.

Walk by Your Side

Many people attempt to teach a dog to heel by putting him on a leash and physically correcting the dog when he makes mistakes. There are a number of things seriously wrong with this approach, the first being that most people do not want precision heeling; rather, they simply want the dog to follow or walk by their side. Second, when physically restrained during "training," even though the dog may grudgingly mope by your side when "handcuffed" on leash, let's see what happens when he is off leash. History! The dog is in the next county because he never enjoyed walking with you on leash and you have no control over him off leash. So let's just teach the dog off leash from the outset to *want* to walk with us. Third, if the dog has not been trained to heel, it is a trifle hasty to think about punishing the poor dog for making mistakes and breaking heeling rules he didn't even know existed. This is simply not fair! Surely, if the dog had been adequately taught how to heel, he would seldom make mistakes and hence there would be no need to correct the dog. Remember, each mistake and each correction (punishment) advertise the trainer's inadequacy, not the dog's. The dog is not stubborn, he is not stupid and he is not bad. Even if he were, he would still require training, so let's train him properly.

Let's teach the dog to *enjoy* following us and to *want* to walk by our side offleash. Then it will be easier to teach high-precision off-leash heeling patterns if desired. After attaching the leash for safety on outdoor walks, but before going anywhere, it is necessary to teach the dog specifically not to pull. Now it will be much easier to teach on-leash walking and heeling because the dog already wants to walk with you, he is familiar with the desired walking and heeling positions and he knows not to pull.

FOLLOWING

Start by training your dog to follow you. Many puppies will follow if you simply walk away from them and maybe click your fingers or chuckle. Adult dogs may require additional enticement to stimulate them to follow, such as a training lure or, at the very least, a lively trainer. To teach the dog to follow: (1) keep walking and (2) walk away from the dog. If the dog attempts to lead or lag, change pace; slow down if the dog forges too far ahead, but speed up if he lags too far behind. Say "Steady!" or "Easy!" each time before you slow down and "Quickly!" or "Hustle!" each time before you speed up, and the dog will learn to change pace on cue. If the dog lags or leads too far, or if he wanders right or left, simply walk quickly in the opposite direction and maybe even run away from the dog and hide.

Practicing is a lot of fun; you can set up a course in your home, yard or park to do this. Indoors, entice the dog to follow upstairs, into a bedroom, into the bathroom, downstairs, around the living room couch, zigzagging between dining room chairs and into the kitchen for dinner. Outdoors, get the dog to follow around park benches, trees, shrubs and along walkways and lines in the grass. (For safety outdoors, it is advisable to attach a long line on the dog, but never exert corrective tension on the line.)

Remember, following has a lot to do with attitude—*your* attitude! Most probably your dog will *not* want to follow Mr. Grumpy Troll with the personality of wilted lettuce. Lighten up—walk with a jaunty step, whistle a happy tune, sing, skip and tell jokes to your dog and he will be right there by your side.

BY YOUR SIDE

It is smart to train the dog to walk close on one side or the other—either side will do, your choice. When walking, jogging or cycling, it is generally bad news to have the dog suddenly cut in front of you. In fact, I train my dogs to walk "By my side" and "Other side"—both very useful instructions. It is possible to position the dog fairly accurately by looking to the appropriate side and clicking your fingers or slapping your thigh on that side. A precise positioning may be attained by holding a training lure, such as a chewtoy, tennis ball, or food treat. Stop and stand still several times throughout the walk, just as you would when window shopping or meeting a friend. Use the lure to make sure the dog slows down and stays close whenever you stop.

When teaching the dog to heel, we generally want her to sit in heel position when we stop. Teach heel

Using a toy to teach sit-heel-sit sequences: 1) "Phoenix, heel!" Standing still, move lure up and back over dog's muzzle.... 2) To position dog sitting in heel position on your left side. 3) "Phoenix, heel!" wagging lure in left hand. Change lure to right hand in preparation for sit signal.

position at the standstill and the dog will learn that the default heel position is sitting by your side (left or right—your choice, unless you wish to compete in obedience trials, in which case the dog must heel on the left).

Several times a day, stand up and call your dog to come and sit in heel position—"Fido, heel!" For example, instruct the dog to come to heel each time there are commercials on TV, or each time you turn a page of a novel, and the dog will get it in a single evening.

Practice straight-line heeling and turns separately. With the dog sitting at heel, teach him to turn in place. After each quarter-turn, half-turn or full turn in place, lure the dog to sit at heel. Now it's time for short straight-line heeling sequences, no more than a few steps at a time. Always think of heeling in terms of Sit-Heel-Sit sequences—start and end with the dog in position and do your best to keep him there when moving. Progressively increase the number of steps in each sequence. When the dog remains close for 20 yards of straight-line heeling, it is time to add a few turns and then sign up for a happy-heeling obedience class to get some advice from the experts.

4) Use hand signal only to lure dog to sit as you stop. Eventually, dog will sit automatically at heel whenever you stop. 5) "Good dog!"

NO PULLING ON LEASH

You can start teaching your dog not to pull on leash anywhere—in front of the television or outdoors—but regardless of location, you must not take a single step with tension in the leash. For a reason known only to dogs, even just a couple of paces of pulling on leash is intrinsically motivating and diabolically rewarding. Instead, attach the leash to the dog's collar, grasp the other end firmly with both hands held close to your chest, and stand still—do not budge an inch. Have somebody watch you with a stopwatch to time your progress, or else you will never believe this will work and so you will not even try the exercise, and your shoulder and the dog's neck will be traumatized for years to come.

Stand still and wait for the dog to stop pulling, and to sit and/or lie down. All dogs stop pulling and sit eventually. Most take only a couple of minutes; the all-time record is 22 ½ minutes. Time how long it takes. Gently praise the dog when he stops pulling, and as soon as he sits, enthusiastically praise the dog and take just one step forwards, then immediately stand still. This single step usually demonstrates the ballistic reinforcing nature of pulling on leash; most dogs explode to the end of the leash, so be prepared for the strain. Stand firm and wait for the dog to sit again. Repeat this half a dozen times and you will probably notice a progressive reduction in the force of the dog's one-step explosions and a radical reduction in the time it takes for the dog to sit each time.

As the dog learns "Sit we go" and "Pull we stop," she will begin to walk forward calmly with each single step and automatically sit when you stop. Now try two steps before you stop. Wooooooo! Scary! When the dog has mastered two steps at a time, try for three. After each success, progressively increase the number of steps in the sequence: try four steps and then six, eight, ten and twenty steps before stopping. Congratulations! You are now walking the dog on leash.

Whenever walking with the dog (off leash or on leash), make sure you stop periodically to practice a few position commands and stays before instructing the dog to "Walk on!" (Remember, you want the dog to be compliant everywhere, not just in the kitchen when his dinner is at hand.) For example, stopping every 25 yards to briefly train the dog amounts to over 200 training interludes within a single three-mile stroll. And each training session is in a different location. You will not believe the improvement within just the first mile of the first walk.

To put it another way, integrating training into a walk offers 200 separate opportunities to use the continuance of the walk as a reward to reinforce the dog's education. Moreover, some training interludes may comprise continuing education for the dog's walking skills: Alternate short periods of the dog walking calmly by your side with periods when the dog is allowed to sniff and investigate the environment. Now sniffing odors on the grass and meeting other dogs become rewards which reinforce the dog's calm and mannerly demeanor. Good Lord! Whatever next? Many enjoyable walks together of course. Happy trails!

THE IMPORTANCE OF TRICKS

Nothing will improve a dog's quality of life better than having a few tricks under its belt. Teaching any trick expands the dog's vocabulary, which facilitates communication and improves the owner's control. Also, specific tricks help prevent and resolve specific behavior problems. For example, by teaching the dog to fetch his toys, the dog learns carrying a toy makes the owner happy and, therefore, will be more likely to chew his toy than other inappropriate items.

More important, teaching tricks prompts owners to lighten up and train with a sunny disposition. Really, tricks should be no different from any other behaviors we put on cue. But they are. When teaching tricks, owners have a much sweeter attitude, which in turn motivates the dog and improves her willingness to comply. The dog feels tricks are a blast, but formal commands are a drag. In fact, tricks are so enjoyable, they may be used as rewards in training by asking the dog to come, sit and down-stay and then rollover for a tummy rub. Go on, try it: Crack a smile and even giggle when the dog promptly and willingly lies down and stays.

Most important, performing tricks prompts onlookers to smile and giggle. Many people are scared of dogs, especially large ones. And nothing can be more off-putting for a dog than to be constantly confronted by strangers who don't like him because of his size or the way he looks. Uneasy people put the dog on edge, causing him to back off and bark, only frightening people all the more. And so a vicious circle develops, with the people's fear fueling the dog's fear *and vice versa*. Instead, tie a pink ribbon to your dog's collar and practice all sorts of tricks on walks and in the park, and you will be pleasantly amazed how it changes people's attitudes toward your friendly dog. The dog's repertoire of tricks is limited only by the trainer's imagination. Below I have described three of my favorites:

SPEAK AND SHUSH

The training sequence involved in teaching a dog to bark on request is no different from that used when training any behavior on cue: request—lure—response—reward. As always, the secret of success lies in finding an effective lure. If the dog always barks at the doorbell, for example, say "Rover, speak!", have an accomplice ring the doorbell, then reward the dog for barking. After a few woofs, ask Rover to "Shush!", waggle a food treat under his nose (to entice him to sniff and thus to shush), praise him when quiet and eventually offer the treat as a reward. Alternate "Speak" and "Shush," progressively increasing the length of shush-time between each barking bout.

PLAYBOW

With the dog standing, say "Bow!" and lower the food lure (palm upwards) to rest between the dog's forepaws. Praise as the dog lowers

her forequarters and sternum to the ground (as when teaching the down), but then lure the dog to stand and offer the treat. On successive trials, gradually increase the length of time the dog is required to remain in the playbow posture in order to gain a food reward. If the dog's rear end collapses into a down, say nothing and offer no reward; simply start over.

BE A BEAR

With the dog sitting backed into a corner to prevent him from toppling over backwards, say "Be a Bear!" With bent paw and palm down, raise a lure upwards and backwards along the top of the dog's muzzle. Praise the dog when he sits up on his haunches and offer the treat as a reward. To prevent the dog from standing on his hind legs, keep the lure closer to the dog's muzzle. On each trial, progressively increase the length of time the dog is required to sit up to receive a food reward. Since lure/reward training is so easy, teach the dog to stand and walk on his hind legs as well!

Teaching "Be a Bear"

chapter 9

Getting
Active
with your Dog

by Bardi McLennan

Once you and your dog have graduated from basic obedience training and are beginning to work together as a team, you can take part in the growing world of dog activities. There are so many fun things to do with your dog! Just remember, people and dogs don't always learn at the same pace, so don't be upset if you (or your dog) need more than two basic training courses before your team becomes operational. Even smart dogs don't go straight to college from kindergarten!

Just as there are events geared to certain types of dogs, so there are ones that are more appealing to certain types of people. In some

128

activities, you give the commands and your dog does the work (upland game hunting is one example), while in others, such as agility, you'll both get a workout. You may want to aim for prestigious titles to add to your dog's name, or you may want nothing more than the sheer enjoyment of being around other people and their dogs. Passive or active, participation has its own rewards.

All dogs seem to love playing flyball.

Consider your dog's physical capabilities when looking into any of the canine activities. It's easy to see that a Basset Hound is not built for the racetrack, nor would a Chihuahua be the breed of choice for pulling a sled. A loyal dog will attempt almost anything you ask him to do, so it is up to you to know your dog's limitations. A dog must be physically sound in order to compete at any level in athletic activities, and being mentally sound is a definite plus. Advanced age, however, may not be a deterrent. Many dogs still hunt and herd at ten or twelve years of age. It's entirely possible for dogs to be "fit at 50." Take your dog for a checkup, explain to your vet the type of activity you have in mind and be guided by his or her findings.

You needn't be restricted to breed-specific sports if it's only fun you're after. Certain AKC activities are limited to designated breeds; however, as each new trial, test or sport has grown in popularity, so has the variety of breeds encouraged to participate at a fun level.

But don't shortchange your fun, or that of your dog, by thinking only of the basic function of her breed. Once a dog has learned how to learn, she can be taught to do just about anything as long as the size of the dog is right for the job and you both think it is fun and rewarding. In other words, you are a team.

To get involved in any of the activities detailed in this chapter, look for the names and addresses of the organizations that sponsor them in Chapter 13. You can also ask your breeder or a local dog trainer for contacts.

You can compete in obedience trials with a well trained dog.

Official American Kennel Club Activities

The following tests and trials are some of the events sanctioned by the AKC and sponsored by various dog clubs. Your dog's expertise will be rewarded with impressive titles. You can participate just for fun, or be competitive and go for those awards.

OBEDIENCE

Training classes begin with pups as young as three months of age in kindergarten puppy training, then advance to pre-novice (all exercises on lead) and go on to novice, which is where you'll start off-lead work. In obedience classes dogs learn to sit, stay, heel and come through a variety of exercises. Once you've got the basics down, you can enter obedience trials and work toward earning your dog's first degree, a C.D. (Companion Dog).

The next level is called "Open," in which jumps and retrieves perk up the dog's interest. Passing grades in competition at this level earn a C.D.X. (Companion Dog Excellent). Beyond that lies the goal of the most ambitious—Utility (U.D. and even U.D.X. or OTCh, an Obedience Champion).

AGILITY

All dogs can participate in the latest canine sport to have gained worldwide popularity for its fun and excitement, agility. It began in England as a canine version of horse show-jumping, but because dogs are more agile and able to perform on verbal commands, extra feats were added such as climbing, balancing and racing through tunnels or in and out of weave poles. Many of the obstacles (regulation or homemade) can be set up in your own backyard. If the agility bug bites, you could end up in international competition!

For starters, your dog should be obedience trained, even though, in the beginning, the lessons may all be taught on lead. Once the dog understands the commands (and you do, too), it's as easy as guiding the dog over a prescribed course, one obstacle at a time. In competition, the race is against the clock, so wear your running shoes! The dog starts with 200 points and the judge deducts for infractions and misadventures along the way.

All dogs seem to love agility and respond to it as if they were being turned loose in a playground paradise. Your dog's enthusiasm will be contagious; agility turns into great fun for dog and owner.

FIELD TRIALS AND HUNTING TESTS

There are field trials and hunting tests for the sporting breeds—retrievers, spaniels and pointing breeds, and for some hounds—Bassets, Beagles and Dachshunds. Field trials are competitive events that test a dog's ability to perform the functions for which she was bred. Hunting tests, which are open to retrievers,

---

TITLES AWARDED BY THE AKC

Conformation: Ch. (Champion)

Obedience: CD (Companion Dog); CDX (Companion Dog Excellent); UD (Utility Dog); UDX (Utility Dog Excellent); OTCh. (Obedience Trial Champion)

Field: JH (Junior Hunter); SH (Senior Hunter); MH (Master Hunter); AFCh. (Amateur Field Champion); FCh. (Field Champion)

Lure Coursing: JC (Junior Courser); SC (Senior Courser)

Herding: HT (Herding Tested); PT (Pre-Trial Tested); HS (Herding Started); HI (Herding Intermediate); HX (Herding Excellent); HCh. (Herding Champion)

Tracking: TD (Tracking Dog); TDX (Tracking Dog Excellent)

Agility: NAD (Novice Agility); OAD (Open Agility); ADX (Agility Excellent); MAX (Master Agility)

Earthdog Tests: JE (Junior Earthdog); SE (Senior Earthdog); ME (Master Earthdog)

Canine Good Citizen: CGC

Combination: DC (Dual Champion—Ch. and Fch.); TC (Triple Champion—Ch., Fch., and OTCh.)

spaniels and pointing breeds only, are noncompetitive and are a means of judging the dog's ability as well as that of the handler.

Hunting is a very large and complex part of canine sports, and if you own one of the breeds that hunts, the events are a great treat for your dog and you. He gets to do what he was bred for, and you get to work with him and watch him do it. You'll be proud of and amazed at what your dog can do.

Fortunately, the AKC publishes a series of booklets on these events, which outline the rules and regulations and include a glossary of the sometimes complicated terms. The AKC also publishes newsletters for field trialers and hunting test enthusiasts. The United Kennel Club (UKC) also has informative materials for the hunter and his dog.

Retrievers and other sporting breeds get to do what they're bred to in hunting tests.

HERDING TESTS AND TRIALS

Herding, like hunting, dates back to the first known uses man made of dogs. The interest in herding today is widespread, and if you own a herding breed, you can join in the activity. Herding dogs are tested for their natural skills to keep a flock of ducks, sheep or cattle together. If your dog shows potential, you can start at the testing level, where your dog can earn a title for showing an inherent herding ability. With training you can advance to the trial level, where your dog should be capable of controlling even difficult livestock in diverse situations.

LURE COURSING

The AKC Tests and Trials for Lure Coursing are open to traditional sighthounds—Greyhounds, Whippets,

Borzoi, Salukis, Afghan Hounds, Ibizan Hounds and
Scottish Deerhounds—as well as to Basenjis and
Rhodesian Ridgebacks. Hounds are judged on overall
ability, follow, speed, agility and endurance. This is possibly the most exciting of the trials for spectators,
because the speed and agility of the dogs is awesome to
watch as they chase the lure (or "course") in heats of
two or three dogs at a time.

TRACKING

*This tracking
dog is hot on
the trail.*

Tracking is another activity in which almost any dog
can compete because
every dog that sniffs the
ground when taken out-
doors is, in fact, tracking.
The hard part comes
when the rules as to what,
when and where the dog
tracks are determined by a
person, not the dog!
Tracking tests cover a
large area of fields, woods
and roads. The tracks are
laid hours before the dogs go to work on them, and
include "tricks" like cross-tracks and sharp turns. If
you're interested in search-and-rescue work, this is the
place to start.

EARTHDOG TESTS FOR SMALL TERRIERS
AND DACHSHUNDS

These tests are open to Australian, Bedlington, Border,
Cairn, Dandie Dinmont, Smooth and Wire Fox,
Lakeland, Norfolk, Norwich, Scottish, Sealyham, Skye,
Welsh and West Highland White Terriers as well as
Dachshunds. The dogs need no prior training for this
terrier sport. There is a qualifying test on the day of
the event, so dog and handler learn the rules on the
spot. These tests, or "digs," sometimes end with infor-
mal races in the late afternoon.

Here are some of the extracurricular obedience and racing activities that are not regulated by the AKC or UKC, but are generally run by clubs or a group of dog fanciers and are often open to all.

Canine Freestyle This activity is something new on the scene and is variously likened to dancing, dressage or ice skating. It is meant to show the athleticism of the dog, but also requires showmanship on the part of the dog's handler. If you and your dog like to ham it up for friends, you might want to look into freestyle.

Lure coursing lets sighthounds do what they do best—run!

Scent Hurdle Racing Scent hurdle racing is purely a fun activity sponsored by obedience clubs with members forming competing teams. The height of the hurdles is based on the size of the shortest dog on the team. On a signal, one team dog is released on each of two side-by-side courses and must clear every hurdle before picking up its own dumbbell from a platform and returning over the jumps to the handler. As each dog returns, the next on that team is sent. Of course, that is what the dogs are supposed to do. When the dogs improvise (going under or around the hurdles, stealing another dog's dumbbell, and so forth), it no doubt frustrates the handlers, but just adds to the fun for everyone else.

Flyball This type of racing is similar, but after negotiating the four hurdles, the dog comes to a flyball box, steps on a lever that releases a tennis ball into the air, catches the ball and returns over the hurdles to the starting point. This game also becomes extremely fun for spectators because the dogs sometimes cheat by catching a ball released by the dog in the next lane. Three titles can be earned—Flyball Dog (F.D.), Flyball Dog Excellent (F.D.X.) and Flyball Dog Champion (Fb.D.Ch.)—all awarded by the North American Flyball Association, Inc.

Dogsledding The name conjures up the Rocky Mountains or the frigid North, but you can find dogsled clubs in such unlikely spots as Maryland, North Carolina and Virginia! Dogsledding is primarily for the Nordic breeds such as the Alaskan Malamutes, Siberian Huskies and Samoyeds, but other breeds can try. There are some practical backyard applications to this sport, too. With parental supervision, almost any strong dog could pull a child's sled.

Coming over the A-frame on an agility course.

These are just some of the many recreational ways you can get to know and understand your multifaceted dog better and have fun doing it.

chapter 10

Your Dog
and your
Family

by Bardi McLennan

Adding a dog automatically increases your family by one, no matter whether you live alone in an apartment or are part of a mother, father and six kids household. The single-person family is fair game for numerous and varied canine misconceptions as to who is dog and who pays the bills, whereas a dog in a houseful of children will consider himself to be just one of the gang, littermates all. One dog and one child may give a dog reason to believe they are both kids or both dogs.

Either interpretation requires parental supervision and sometimes speedy intervention.

As soon as one paw goes through the door into your home, Rufus (or Rufina) has to make many adjustments to become a part of your family. Your job is to make him fit in as painlessly as possible. An older dog may have some frame of reference from past experience, but to a 10-week-old puppy, everything is brand new: people, furniture, stairs, when and where people eat, sleep or watch TV, his own place and everyone else's space, smells, sounds, outdoors—everything!

Puppies, and newly acquired dogs of any age, do not need what we think of as "freedom." If you leave a new dog or puppy loose in the house, you will almost certainly return to chaotic destruction and the dog will forever after equate your homecoming with a time of punishment to be dreaded. It is unfair to give your dog what amounts to "freedom to get into trouble." Instead, confine him to a crate for brief periods of your absence (up to three or four hours) and, for the long haul, a workday for example, confine him to one untrashable area with his own toys, a bowl of water and a radio left on (low) in another room.

Lots of pets get along with each other just fine.

For the first few days, when not confined, put Rufus on a long leash tied to your wrist or waist. This umbilical cord method enables the dog to learn all about you from your body language and voice, and to learn by his own actions which things in the house are NO! and which ones are rewarded by "Good dog." House-training will be easier with the pup always by your side. Speaking of which, accidents do happen. That goal of "completely housetrained" takes up to a year, or the length of time it takes the pup to mature.

The All-Adult Family

Most dogs in an adults-only household today are likely to be latchkey pets, with no one home all day but the dog. When you return after a tough day on the job, the dog can and should be your relaxation therapy. But going home can instead be a daily frustration.

Separation anxiety is a very common problem for the dog in a working household. It may begin with whines and barks of loneliness, but it will soon escalate into a frenzied destruction derby. That is why it is so important to set aside the time to teach a dog to relax when left alone in his confined area and to understand that he can trust you to return.

Let the dog get used to your work schedule in easy stages. Confine him to one room and go in and out of that room over and over again. Be casual about it. No physical, voice or eye contact. When the pup no longer even notices your comings and goings, leave the house for varying lengths of time, returning to stay home for a few minutes and gradually increasing the time away. This training can take days, but the dog is learning that you haven't left him forever and that he can trust you.

Any time you leave the dog, but especially during this training period, be casual about your departure. No anxiety-building fond farewells. Just "Bye" and go! Remember the "Good dog" when you return to find everything more or less as you left it.

If things are a mess (or even a disaster) when you return, greet the dog, take him outside to eliminate, and then put him in his crate while you clean up. Rant and rave in the shower! *Do not* punish the dog. You were not there when it happened, and the rule is: Only punish as you catch the dog in the act of wrongdoing. Obviously, it makes sense to get your latchkey puppy when you'll have a week or two to spend on these training essentials.

Family weekend activities should include Rufus whenever possible. Depending on the pup's age, now is the time for a long walk in the park, playtime in the backyard, a hike in the woods. Socializing is as important as health care, good food and physical exercise, so visiting Aunt Emma or Uncle Harry and the next-door neighbor's dog or cat is essential to developing an outgoing, friendly temperament in your pet.

If you are a single adult, socializing Rufus at home and away will prevent him from becoming overly protective of you (or just overly attached) and will also prevent such behavioral problems as dominance or fear of strangers.

Babies

Whether already here or on the way, babies figure larger than life in the eyes of a dog. If the dog is there first, let him in on all your baby preparations in the house. When baby arrives, let Rufus sniff any item of clothing that has been on the baby before Junior comes home. Then let Mom greet the dog first before introducing the new family member. Hold the baby down for the dog to see and sniff, but make sure someone's holding the dog on lead in case of any sudden moves. Don't play keep-away or tease the dog with the baby, which only invites undesirable jumping up.

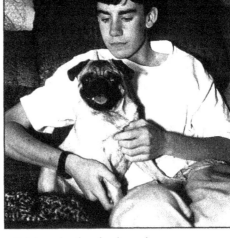

The dog and the baby are "family," and for starters can be treated almost as equals. Things rapidly change, however, especially when baby takes to creeping around on all fours on the dog's turf or, better yet, has yummy pudding all over her face and hands! That's when a lot of things in the dog's and baby's lives become more separate than equal.

Dogs are perfect confidants.

Toddlers make terrible dog owners, but if you can't avoid the combination, use patient discipline (that is, positive teaching rather than punishment), and use time-outs before you run out of patience.

A dog and a baby (or toddler, or an assertive young child) should never be left alone together. Take the dog with you or confine him. With a baby or youngsters in the house, you'll have plenty of use for that wonderful canine safety device called a crate!

Young Children

Any dog in a house with kids will behave pretty much as the kids do, good or bad. But even good dogs and good children can get into trouble when play becomes rowdy and active.

Legs bobbing up and down, shrill voices screeching, a ball hurtling overhead, all add up to exuberant frustration for a dog who's just trying to be part of the gang. In a pack of puppies, any legs or toys being chased would be caught by a set of teeth, and all the pups involved would understand that is how the game is played. Kids do not understand this, nor do parents tolerate it. Bring Rufus indoors before you have reason to regret it. This is time-out, not a punishment.

Teach children how to play nicely with a puppy.

You can explain the situation to the children and tell them they must play quieter games until the puppy learns not to grab them with his mouth. Unfortunately, you can't explain it that easily to the dog. With adult supervision, they will learn how to play together.

Young children love to tease. Sticking their faces or wiggling their hands or fingers in the dog's face is teasing. To another person it might be just annoying, but it is threatening to a dog. There's another difference: We can make the child stop by an explanation, but the only way a dog can stop it is with a warning growl and then with teeth. Teasing is the major cause of children being bitten by their pets. Treat it seriously.

Older Children

The best age for a child to get a first dog is between the ages of 8 and 12. That's when kids are able to accept some real responsibility for their pet. Even so, take the child's vow of "I will never *ever* forget to feed (brush, walk, etc.) the dog" for what it's worth: a child's good intention at that moment. Most kids today have extra lessons, soccer practice, Little League, ballet, and so forth piled on top of school schedules. There will be many times when Mom will have to come to the dog's rescue. "I walked the dog for you so you can set the table for me" is one way to get around a missed appointment without laying on blame or guilt.

Kids in this age group make excellent obedience trainers because they are into the teaching/learning process themselves and they lack the self-consciousness of adults. Attending a dog show is something the whole family can enjoy, and watching Junior Showmanship may catch the eye of the kids. Older children can begin to get involved in many of the recreational activities that were reviewed in the previous chapter. Some of the agility obstacles, for example, can be set up in the backyard as a family project (with an adult making sure all the equipment is safe and secure for the dog).

Older kids are also beginning to look to the future, and may envision themselves as veterinarians or trainers or show dog handlers or writers of the next Lassie best-seller. Dogs are perfect confidants for these dreams. They won't tell a soul.

Other Pets

Introduce all pets tactfully. In a dog/cat situation, hold the dog, not the cat. Let two dogs meet on neutral turf—a stroll in the park or a walk down the street—with both on loose leads to permit all the normal canine ways of saying hello, including routine sniffing, circling, more sniffing, and so on. Small creatures such as hamsters, chinchillas or mice must be kept safe from their natural predators (dogs and cats).

Festive Family Occasions

Parties are great for people, but not necessarily for puppies. Until all the guests have arrived, put the dog in his crate or in a room where he won't be disturbed. A socialized dog can join the fun later as long as he's not underfoot, annoying guests or into the hors d'oeuvres.

There are a few dangers to consider, too. Doors opening and closing can allow a puppy to slip out unnoticed in the confusion, and you'll be organizing a search party instead of playing host or hostess. Party food and buffet service are not for dogs. Let Rufus party in his crate with a nice big dog biscuit.

At Christmas time, not only are tree decorations dangerous and breakable (and perhaps family heirlooms), but extreme caution should be taken with the lights, cords and outlets for the tree lights and any other festive lighting. Occasionally a dog lifts a leg, ignoring the fact that the tree is indoors. To avoid this, use a canine repellent, made for gardens, on the tree. Or keep him out of the tree room unless supervised. And whatever you do, *don't* invite trouble by hanging his toys on the tree!

Car Travel

Before you plan a vacation by car or RV with Rufus, be sure he enjoys car travel. Nothing spoils a holiday quicker than a carsick dog! Work within the dog's comfort level. Get in the car with the dog in his crate or attached to a canine car safety belt and just sit there until he relaxes. That's all. Next time, get in the car, turn on the engine and go nowhere. Just sit. When that is okay, turn on the engine and go around the block. Now you can go for a ride and include a stop where you get out, leaving the dog for a minute or two.

On a warm day, always park in the shade and leave windows open several inches. And return quickly. It only takes 10 minutes for a car to become an overheated steel death trap.

Motel or Pet Motel?

Not all motels or hotels accept pets, but you have a much better choice today than even a few years ago. To find a dog-friendly lodging, look at *On the Road Again With Man's Best Friend*, a series of directories that detail bed and breakfasts, inns, family resorts and other hotels/motels. Some places require a refundable deposit to cover any damage incurred by the dog. More B&Bs accept pets now, but some restrict the size.

If taking Rufus with you is not feasible, check out boarding kennels in your area. Your veterinarian may offer this service, or recommend a kennel or two he or she is familiar with. Go see the facilities for yourself, ask about exercise, diet, housing, and so on. Or, if you'd rather have Rufus stay home, look into bonded petsitters, many of whom will also bring in the mail and water your plants.

chapter 11

Your Dog
and your
Community

by Bardi McLennan

Step outside your home with your dog and you are no longer just family, you are both part of your community. This is when the phrase "responsible pet ownership" takes on serious implications. For starters, it means you pick up after your dog—not just occasionally, but every time your dog eliminates away from home. That means you have joined the Plastic Baggy Brigade! You always have plastic sandwich bags in your pocket and several in the car. It means you teach your kids how to use them, too. If you think this is "yucky," just imagine what

the person (a non-doggy person) who inadvertently steps in the mess thinks!

Your responsibility extends to your neighbors: To their ears (no annoying barking); to their property (their garbage, their lawn, their flower beds, their cat— especially their cat); to their kids (on bikes, at play); to their kids' toys and sports equipment.

There are numerous dog-related laws, ranging from simple dog licensing and leash laws to those holding you liable for any physical injury or property damage done by your dog. These laws are in place to protect everyone in the community, including you and your dog. There are town ordinances and state laws which are by no means the same in all towns or all states. Ignorance of the law won't get you off the hook. The time to find out what the laws are where you live is now.

Be sure your dog's license is current. This is not just a good local ordinance, it can make the difference between finding your lost dog or not.

Dressing your dog up makes him appealing to strangers.

Many states now require proof of rabies vaccination and that the dog has been spayed or neutered before issuing a license. At the same time, keep up the dog's annual immunizations.

Never let your dog run loose in the neighborhood. This will not only keep you on the right side of the leash law, it's the outdoor version of the rule about not giving your dog "freedom to get into trouble."

Good Canine Citizen

Sometimes it's hard for a dog's owner to assess whether or not the dog is sufficiently socialized to be accepted by the community at large. Does Rufus or Rufina display good, controlled behavior in public? The AKC's Canine Good Citizen program is available through many dog organizations. If your dog passes the test, the title "CGC" is earned.

The overall purpose is to turn your dog into a good neighbor and to teach you about your responsibility to your community as a dog owner. Here are the ten things your dog must do willingly:

1. Accept a stranger stopping to chat with you.
2. Sit and be petted by a stranger.
3. Allow a stranger to handle him or her as a groomer or veterinarian would.
4. Walk nicely on a loose lead.
5. Walk calmly through a crowd.
6. Sit and down on command, then stay in a sit or down position while you walk away.
7. Come when called.
8. Casually greet another dog.
9. React confidently to distractions.
10. Accept being left alone with someone other than you and not become overly agitated or nervous.

Schools and Dogs

Schools are getting involved with pet ownership on an educational level. It has been proven that children who are kind to animals are humane in their attitude toward other people as adults.

A dog is a child's best friend, and so children are often primary pet owners, if not the primary caregivers. Unfortunately, they are also the ones most often bitten by dogs. This occurs due to a lack of understanding that pets, no matter how sweet, cuddly and loving, are still animals. Schools, along with parents, dog clubs, dog fanciers and the AKC, are working to change all that with video programs for children not only in grade school, but in the nursery school and pre-kindergarten age group. Teaching youngsters how to be responsible dog owners is important community work. When your dog has a CGC, volunteer to take part in an educational classroom event put on by your dog club.

Boy Scout Merit Badge

A Merit Badge for Dog Care can be earned by any Boy
Scout ages 11 to 18. The requirements are not easy, but
amount to a complete course in responsible dog care
and general ownership. Here are just a few of the
things a Scout must do to earn that badge:

> Point out ten parts of the dog using the correct
> names.

> Give a report (signed by parent or guardian) on
> your care of the dog (feeding, food used, housing,
> exercising, grooming and bathing), plus what has
> been done to keep the dog healthy.

> Explain the right way to obedience train a dog,
> and demonstrate three comments.

> Several of the requirements have to do with health
> care, including first aid, handling a hurt dog, and
> the dangers of home treatment for a serious
> ailment.

> The final requirement is to know the local laws
> and ordinances involving dogs.

There are similar programs for Girl Scouts and 4-H
members.

Local Clubs

Local dog clubs are no longer in existence just to put
on a yearly dog show. Today, they are apt to be the hub
of the community's involvement with pets. Dog clubs
conduct educational forums with big-name speakers,
stage demonstrations of canine talent in a busy mall
and take dogs of various breeds to schools for classroom discussion.

The quickest way to feel accepted as a member in a
club is to volunteer your services! Offer to help with
something—anything—and watch your popularity
(and your interest) grow.

Therapy Dogs

Once your dog has earned that essential CGC and reliably demonstrates a steady, calm temperament, you could look into what therapy dogs are doing in your area.

Therapy dogs go with their owners to visit patients at hospitals or nursing homes, generally remaining on leash but able to coax a pat from a stiffened hand, a smile from a blank face, a few words from sealed lips or a hug from someone in need of love.

Nursing homes cover a wide range of patient care. Some specialize in care of the elderly, some in the treatment of specific illnesses, some in physical therapy. Children's facilities also welcome visits from trained therapy dogs for boosting morale in their pediatric patients. Hospice care for the terminally ill and the at-home care of AIDS patients are other areas where this canine visiting is desperately needed. Therapy dog training comes first.

Your dog can make a difference in lots of lives.

There is a lot more involved than just taking your nice friendly pooch to someone's bedside. Doing therapy dog work involves your own emotional stability as well as that of your dog. But once you have met all the requirements for this work, making the rounds once a week or once a month with your therapy dog is possibly the most rewarding of all community activities.

Disaster Aid

This community service is definitely not for everyone, partly because it is time-consuming. The initial training is rigorous, and there can be no let-up in the continuing workouts, because members are on call 24 hours a day to go wherever they are needed at a moment's notice. But if you think you would like to be able to assist in a disaster, look into search-and-rescue work. The network of search-and-rescue volunteers is worldwide, and all members of the American Rescue Dog Association (ARDA) who are qualified to do this work are volunteers who train and maintain their own dogs.

Physical Aid

Most people are familiar with Seeing Eye dogs, which serve as blind people's eyes, but not with all the other work that dogs are trained to do to assist the disabled. Dogs are also specially trained to pull wheelchairs, carry school books, pick up dropped objects, open and close doors. Some also are ears for the deaf. All these assistance-trained dogs, by the way, are allowed anywhere "No Pet" signs exist (as are therapy dogs when

Making the rounds with your therapy dog can be very rewarding.

properly identified). Getting started in any of this fascinating work requires a background in dog training and canine behavior, but there are also volunteer jobs ranging from answering the phone to cleaning out kennels to providing a foster home for a puppy. You have only to ask.

part four

Beyond
the
Basics

chapter 12

Recommended Reading

Books

ABOUT HEALTH CARE

Ackerman, Lowell. *Guide to Skin and Haircoat Problems in Dogs.* Loveland, Colo.: Alpine Publications, 1994.

Alderton, David. *The Dog Care Manual.* Hauppauge, N.Y.: Barron's Educational Series, Inc., 1986.

American Kennel Club. *American Kennel Club Dog Care and Training.* New York: Howell Book House, 1991.

Bamberger, Michelle, DVM. *Help! The Quick Guide to First Aid for Your Dog.* New York: Howell Book House, 1995.

Carlson, Delbert, DVM, and James Giffin, MD. *Dog Owner's Home Veterinary Handbook.* New York: Howell Book House, 1992.

DeBitetto, James, DVM, and Sarah Hodgson. *You & Your Puppy.* New York: Howell Book House, 1995.

Humphries, Jim, DVM. *Dr. Jim's Animal Clinic for Dogs.* New York: Howell Book House, 1994.

McGinnis, Terri. *The Well Dog Book.* New York: Random House, 1991.

Pitcairn, Richard and Susan. *Natural Health for Dogs.* Emmaus, Pa.: Rodale Press, 1982.

ABOUT DOG SHOWS

Hall, Lynn. *Dog Showing for Beginners.* New York: Howell Book House, 1994.

Nichols, Virginia Tuck. *How to Show Your Own Dog.* Neptune, N. J.: TFH, 1970.

Vanacore, Connie. *Dog Showing, An Owner's Guide.* New York: Howell Book House, 1990.

About Training

Ammen, Amy. *Training in No Time*. New York: Howell Book House, 1995.

Baer, Ted. *Communicating With Your Dog*. Hauppauge, N.Y.: Barron's Educational Series, Inc., 1989.

Benjamin, Carol Lea. *Dog Problems*. New York: Howell Book House, 1989.

Benjamin, Carol Lea. *Dog Training for Kids*. New York: Howell Book House, 1988.

Benjamin, Carol Lea. *Mother Knows Best*. New York: Howell Book House, 1985.

Benjamin, Carol Lea. *Surviving Your Dog's Adolescence*. New York: Howell Book House, 1993.

Bohnenkamp, Gwen. *Manners for the Modern Dog*. San Francisco: Perfect Paws, 1990.

Dibra, Bashkim. *Dog Training by Bash*. New York: Dell, 1992.

Dunbar, Ian, PhD, MRCVS. *Dr. Dunbar's Good Little Dog Book*, James & Kenneth Publishers, 2140 Shattuck Ave. #2406, Berkeley, Calif. 94704. (510) 658–8588. Order from the publisher.

Dunbar, Ian, PhD, MRCVS. *How to Teach a New Dog Old Tricks*, James & Kenneth Publishers. Order from the publisher; address above.

Dunbar, Ian, PhD, MRCVS, and Gwen Bohnenkamp. Booklets on *Preventing Aggression; Housetraining; Chewing; Digging; Barking; Socialization; Fearfulness; and Fighting*, James & Kenneth Publishers. Order from the publisher; address above.

Evans, Job Michael. *People, Pooches and Problems*. New York: Howell Book House, 1991.

Kilcommons, Brian and Sarah Wilson. *Good Owners, Great Dogs*. New York: Warner Books, 1992.

McMains, Joel M. *Dog Logic—Companion Obedience*. New York: Howell Book House, 1992.

Rutherford, Clarice and David H. Neil, MRCVS. *How to Raise a Puppy You Can Live With*. Loveland, Colo.: Alpine Publications, 1982.

Volhard, Jack and Melissa Bartlett. *What All Good Dogs Should Know: The Sensible Way to Train*. New York: Howell Book House, 1991.

About Breeding

Harris, Beth J. Finder. *Breeding a Litter, The Complete Book of Prenatal and Postnatal Care*. New York: Howell Book House, 1983.

Holst, Phyllis, DVM. *Canine Reproduction*. Loveland, Colo.: Alpine Publications, 1985.

Walkowicz, Chris and Bonnie Wilcox, DVM. *Successful Dog Breeding, The Complete Handbook of Canine Midwifery*. New York: Howell Book House, 1994.

ABOUT ACTIVITIES

American Rescue Dog Association. *Search and Rescue Dogs*. New York: Howell Book House, 1991.

Barwig, Susan and Stewart Hilliard. *Schutzhund*. New York: Howell Book House, 1991.

Beaman, Arthur S. *Lure Coursing*. New York: Howell Book House, 1994.

Daniels, Julie. *Enjoying Dog Agility—From Backyard to Competition*. New York: Doral Publishing, 1990.

Davis, Kathy Diamond. *Therapy Dogs*. New York: Howell Book House, 1992.

Gallup, Davis Anne. *Running With Man's Best Friend*. Loveland, Colo.: Alpine Publications, 1986.

Habgood, Dawn and Robert. *On the Road Again With Man's Best Friend*. New England, Mid-Atlantic, West Coast and Southeast editions. Selective guides to area bed and breakfasts, inns, hotels and resorts that welcome guests and their dogs. New York: Howell Book House, 1995.

Holland, Vergil S. *Herding Dogs*. New York: Howell Book House, 1994.

LaBelle, Charlene G. *Backpacking With Your Dog*. Loveland, Colo.: Alpine Publications, 1993.

Simmons-Moake, Jane. *Agility Training, The Fun Sport for All Dogs*. New York: Howell Book House, 1991.

Spencer, James B. *Hup! Training Flushing Spaniels the American Way*. New York: Howell Book House, 1992.

Spencer, James B. *Point! Training the All-Seasons Birddog*. New York: Howell Book House, 1995.

Tarrant, Bill. *Training the Hunting Retriever*. New York: Howell Book House, 1991.

Volhard, Jack and Wendy. *The Canine Good Citizen*. New York: Howell Book House, 1994.

General Titles

Haggerty, Captain Arthur J. *How to Get Your Pet Into Show Business*. New York: Howell Book House, 1994.

McLennan, Bardi. *Dogs and Kids, Parenting Tips*. New York: Howell Book House, 1993.

Moran, Patti J. *Pet Sitting for Profit, A Complete Manual for Professional Success*. New York: Howell Book House, 1992.

Scalisi, Danny and Libby Moses. *When Rover Just Won't Do, Over 2,000 Suggestions for Naming Your Dog.* New York: Howell Book House, 1993.

Sife, Wallace, PhD. *The Loss of a Pet.* New York: Howell Book House, 1993.

Wrede, Barbara J. *Civilizing Your Puppy.* Hauppauge, N.Y.: Barron's Educational Series, 1992.

Magazines

The AKC GAZETTE, The Official Journal for the Sport of Purebred Dogs. American Kennel Club, 51 Madison Ave., New York, NY.

Bloodlines Journal. United Kennel Club, 100 E. Kilgore Rd., Kalamazoo, MI.

Dog Fancy. Fancy Publications, 3 Burroughs, Irvine, CA 92718

Dog World. Maclean Hunter Publishing Corp., 29 N. Wacker Dr., Chicago, IL 60606.

Videos

"SIRIUS Puppy Training," by Ian Dunbar, PhD, MRCVS. James & Kenneth Publishers, 2140 Shattuck Ave. #2406, Berkeley, CA 94704. Order from the publisher.

"Training the Companion Dog," from Dr. Dunbar's British TV Series, James & Kenneth Publishers. (See address above).

The American Kennel Club produces videos on every breed of dog, as well as on hunting tests, field trials and other areas of interest to purebred dog owners. For more information, write to AKC/Video Fulfillment, 5580 Centerview Dr., Suite 200, Raleigh, NC 27606.

chapter 13

Resources

Breed Clubs

Every breed recognized by the American Kennel Club has a national (parent) club. National clubs are a great source of information on your breed. You can get the name of the secretary of the club by contacting:

The American Kennel Club
51 Madison Avenue
New York, NY 10010
(212) 696-8200

There are also numerous all-breed, individual breed, obedience, hunting and other special-interest dog clubs across the country. The American Kennel Club can provide you with a geographical list of clubs to find ones in your area. Contact them at the above address.

Registry Organizations

Registry organizations register purebred dogs. The American Kennel Club is the oldest and largest in this country, and currently recognizes over 130 breeds. The United Kennel Club registers some breeds the AKC doesn't (including the American Pit Bull Terrier and the Miniature Fox Terrier) as well as many of the same breeds. The others included here are for your reference; the AKC can provide you with a list of foreign registries.

American Kennel Club
51 Madison Avenue
New York, NY 10010

United Kennel Club (UKC)
100 E. Kilgore Road
Kalamazoo, MI 49001-5598

American Dog Breeders Assn.
P.O. Box 1771
Salt Lake City, UT 84110
(Registers American Pit Bull Terriers)

Canadian Kennel Club
89 Skyway Avenue
Etobicoke, Ontario
Canada M9W 6R4

National Stock Dog Registry
P.O. Box 402
Butler, IN 46721
(Registers working stock dogs)

Orthopedic Foundation for Animals (OFA)
2300 E. Nifong Blvd.
Columbia, MO 65201-3856
(Hip registry)

Activity Clubs

Write to these organizations for information on the
activities they sponsor.

American Kennel Club
51 Madison Avenue
New York, NY 10010
(Conformation Shows, Obedience Trials, Field
Trials and Hunting Tests, Agility, Canine Good

Citizen, Lure Coursing, Herding, Tracking,
Earthdog Tests, Coonhunting.)

United Kennel Club
100 E. Kilgore Road
Kalamazoo, MI 49001-5598
(Conformation Shows, Obedience Trials, Agility,
Hunting for Various Breeds, Terrier Trials and
more.)

North American Flyball Assn.
1342 Jeff St.
Ypsilanti, MI 48198

International Sled Dog Racing Assn.
P.O. Box 446
Norman, ID 83848-0446

North American Working Dog Assn., Inc.
Southeast Kreisgruppe
P.O. Box 833
Brunswick, GA 31521

Trainers

Association of Pet Dog Trainers
P.O. Box 3734
Salinas, CA 93912
(408) 663–9257

American Dog Trainers' Network
161 West 4th St.
New York, NY 10014
(212) 727–7257

**National Association of Dog Obedience
Instructors**
2286 East Steel Rd.
St. Johns, MI 48879

Associations

American Dog Owners Assn.
1654 Columbia Tpk.
Castleton, NY 12033
(Combats anti-dog legislation)

Delta Society
P.O. Box 1080
Renton, WA 98057-1080
(Promotes the human/animal bond through
pet-assisted therapy and other programs)

Dog Writers Assn. of America (DWAA)
Sally Cooper, Secy.
222 Woodchuck Ln.
Harwinton, CT 06791

National Assn. for Search and Rescue (NASAR)
P.O. Box 3709
Fairfax, VA 22038

Therapy Dogs International
6 Hilltop Road
Mendham, NJ 07945

Printed in the USA
CPSIA information can be obtained
at www.ICGtesting.com
JSHW012011140824
68134JS00023B/2359